WHY ME?
AND NO GOLD WATCH!

Also by Rick Atkinson:

Don't Just Retire — Live It, Love It!
Strategies for Retiring Right!

WHY ME?
AND NO GOLD WATCH!

RICK ATKINSON

INSOMNIAC PRESS

Cover design by Mike O'Connor. Cover image by iStockphoto.com.

Library and Archives Canada Cataloguing in Publication

Title: Why me and no gold watch? : a personal planning guide to
    retirement : creating &
  implementing the best life after work plan / Rick Atkinson.
Names: Atkinson, Richard, 1941- author.
Identifiers: Canadiana (print) 20190100516 | Canadiana (ebook)
    20190100524 | ISBN 9781554832354
  (softcover) | ISBN 9781554832477 (HTML)
Subjects: LCSH: Retirement. | LCSH: Retirement—Planning. | LCSH:
    Retirement—Psychological aspects.
  | LCSH: Retirees—Life skills guides.
Classification: LCC HQ1062 .A85 2019 | DDC 646.7/9—dc23

Printed and bound in Canada

Insomniac Press, 520 Princess Ave.
London, Ontario, Canada, N6B 2B8
www.insomniacpress.com

I dedicate this book to all those who shared their thoughts, concerns, and experiences about life after work. I sincerely thank you for your views, observations, experiences, and recommendations. You have enriched my life and provided me with lessons to pass on to others.

Contents

Introduction		9
Chapter 1 —	Why Me? And No Gold Watch!	17
Chapter 2 —	Getting Ready to Make the Plunge	33
Chapter 3 —	Working and Volunteering As Part of Your Lifestyle	52
Chapter 4 —	The Straight Goods on Money	62
Chapter 5 —	Health and Well-Being	78
Chapter 6 —	The Importance of Spirituality	92
Chapter 7 —	A Positive Attitude Leads to a Longer Retirement	97
Chapter 8 —	Choosing Where to Live	103
Chapter 9 —	The Best Time to Retire	112
Chapter 10 —	Relationships in Retirement	116
Chapter 11 —	Being Remembered: Your Legacy	136
Chapter 12 —	Put Things in Writing	142
Chapter 13 —	Dealing with Fear and Increasing Self-Confidence	146
Chapter 14 —	How to Have Fun	156
Chapter 15 —	Death and Dying	162
Chapter 16 —	Making a Will	166
Chapter 17 —	Finding and Using a Retirement Mentor	179
Chapter 18 —	Examples of Retiring Planning	189
Chapter 19 —	You As a Mentor	197
Chapter 20 —	Pets in Retirement	199

Appendix

Canada Pension Plan/Québec Pension Plan
    (CPP/QPP) — Canada   205
Old Age Security (OAS) — Canada   207
Social Security (US)   207
Company Pension Plans and Benefits   208
Savings Plans, Retirement Accounts, and Other
    Assets   208
Tips for Living on a Budget   209
Caring for Elderly Parents   211
Parenting in Retirement   219
Step-Grandparenting   225
Family Challenges   226
Sex   229
Increasing the Romance   231
Websites for Seniors   235

Introduction

So you're thinking about retirement. Sitting at your desk or standing by your machine, you picture waking up in the morning when you're ready to, instead of when you have to; you lounge around the house with a cup of coffee and your favourite book; you call up friends for tennis or a game of golf or maybe to play cards in the evening. Ah, freedom at last! You're no longer working. You're no longer commuting. For the first time in a long time, you're really enjoying life. Finally, you are retired.

When most people think about retirement, they imagine leaving a job they dislike, dropping out of the rat race, and turning their back on the pressures of employment. They often see retirement as a welcome change or an escape to something more peaceful and serene.

However, retiring is not only about giving up your job and spending your days relaxing; it's also about entering one of the most exciting and challenging stages of life. Retirement can be a time to draw upon your personal and professional experiences to open new doors of opportunity and education. It can be a time to realize your potential and accomplish significant goals that you delayed because of the responsibilities of managing a career and raising a family.

The opportunities in retirement are endless; however, a successful retirement doesn't come without its hurdles. There are many considerations such as living on a reduced income, creating a health and wellness strategy, examining relationships with family and friends, allocating personal time, establishing living arrangements, adopting and adapting to different social roles, and adjusting to the eventual death of a partner, friends, and family members.

In your quest for a successful retirement, beware of retirement's outmoded stereotypes. Retirement used to mean a life in which retirees become non-productive, non-contributing members of society, heading into their final sunset. Many retirees still have this pessimistic view and end up mentally "hanging up their skates." They don't expect much from retirement, and, unfortunately, that's just what they get.

A fourteen-year study of six thousand retired adults living in the US found those who had a purpose in life were more likely to still be around at the end of the fourteen years than those who considered themselves "aimless."

For some people, purpose is connected to vocation — meaningful, satisfying work or volunteering. For others, their purpose lies in responsibilities to family and friends. Others seek meaning through artistic activities or religious beliefs. Some people find their purpose clearly expressed in all these aspects of life.

A Retirement Revolution

The good news is a quiet revolution has been taking place. Today's successful retirees are energized and are actively pursuing new life goals. By adopting a zest for life, no matter their circumstances, they're enthusiastic about the future and they shape their destiny as much as possible.

It's worth noting that the concept of living comfortably after retirement is a fairly new one. US Social Security is only about eighty years old, and the Canada Pension Plan

(CPP) is a little over fifty years young. Before the introduction of these systems, retirement was a luxury of the wealthy. Other people — most people — kept working until they couldn't any longer and often suffered after that point.

After World War II, as the middle class grew, so did the notion of retiring, of living comfortably after one stopped working. This in turn generated the concept of retirement planning.

In the beginning, the general focus of retirement planning was centred on money questions such as "How much will I need to retire comfortably?" "Will the money I've saved last long enough?" and "How much will I be able to pass on to my heirs?" As time went on, many realized that retirement is about much more than money and that planning for our non-monetary needs is also important. We need to plan what we'll do with our time. We also need to consider things such as maintaining or improving our health, and how we'll develop new social circles outside of work.

The importance of these things and more — a holistic approach — has become as vital as the financial issues for one simple reason: We're living longer!

A Central Question and Personal Story

Most of us retiring today will live another fifteen, twenty, thirty, or more years. Retirement could be the second longest period of our life. Considering this fact, I have a question for you:

Will you create the best retirement you can, or will you let your retirement years just happen to you?

Letting retirement just happen is exactly what many people do to the detriment of themselves and their loved ones. Let me share a personal story that illustrates the dangers of retiring without a well-thought-out plan.

My father, Jack Atkinson, was more than merely successful in his work. He loved his job. His friends were there. His self-image was part of the job. His life happily revolved around work until the day he retired.

My father didn't have any hobbies or interests outside of his work. Like many others, his mental, physical, and emotional well-being was set adrift when he no longer had a job to go to. Eighteen months later, he passed away.

Naturally, this left a big impression on me. I was only twenty-four at the time and just starting my human resources career. Over the years, as a human resources professional, I observed hundreds of people move from active work to retirement. I eventually came to realize that the difference between thriving and failing to thrive in retirement was not about the money. I sometimes think, "If I knew then what I know now, maybe I could have helped guide Dad's retirement planning to a different end."

Unsuccessful Retirees

Unsuccessful retirees mainly see retirement as an escape. They picture retirement as the time they got rid of a job and/or boss they couldn't stand, finally leaving behind the stress of long commutes and undesirable working conditions. Some unsuccessful retirees are forced into retirement due to the downsizing or outsourcing of their duties and responsibilities. Ill health also can cause earlier retirement. Regardless of the cause, unsuccessful retirees tend to see retirement as a vacation, and they try to fill their days the same way they did when on vacation. Unfortunately, vacation activities become boring — as well as expensive.

After a while, the vacation model fails and retirement no longer feels like an extended holiday. These retirees are then left with little to do that interests or engages them, and time begins to weigh heavily on their shoulders. Many of these retirees experience increased frustration and disappointment with their lives.

The problems these retirees experience are not generated by laziness or apathy. Rather, we can see the root causes in contrast to the factors that make successful retirees.

Successful Retirees

Successful retirees are often glad to leave their job, and they also look forward to having more time for the things they enjoyed when on vacation. Successful retirees can too suffer from downsizing, outsourcing or ill health. However, successful retirees have a clear concept of what makes for a well-rounded, holistic, happy, and stimulated retirement. Many acquire that information from people who are already living a successful retirement. They may have read books and articles on retirement planning and/or attended workshops to learn how best to plan for the rest of their life.

Successful retirees take all their accumulated information and apply it in two ways:

1. **They build their own realistic and well-rounded vision of retirement.**
2. **They create and implement a plan to make it happen.**

This book is designed to assist you in doing the same. It outlines the issues you need to address, and it covers the best practices. It is my intent to provide you with insight and direction without compromising your own decision-making process.

To spotlight the learning, we'll look at Sally McBride, a fifty-seven-year-old employee at Benson & Sons who will be involuntarily leaving her position as a senior marketing associate due to an organizational restructuring. Throughout the book, Sally, her friend Thelma Brooks and others will be referenced to help us explore the knowledge, thoughts and insights I've gleaned from interviews with hundreds of successful retirees.

So now the choice is yours. You can sit and wait for whatever comes along or you can tackle the challenges and opportunities of retiring successfully. Will you reserve your place in the rocking chair or grab the brass ring of retirement life?

If you are somewhere between the ages of forty-five and sixty-five, it's time to explore your future as a retiree. Consider the contents of this book and take time to complete the exercises. Be sure to share your thoughts with your partner as you progress toward developing your personal retirement vision and plan.

If you are already retired, please use the book to add a little more sizzle to your "golden years."

If you are a millennial, the lessons included in these chapters are strategies you may wish to share with your parents — a gift from you in assisting them to a happy and stimulating retirement.

Congratulations on being among those who take a proactive interest in retirement. I wish you all the best in developing a plan that enriches your life.

Kindest regards,

Richard (Rick) Atkinson

Chapter 1

Why Me? And No Gold Watch!

Summary:

Few of us have complete control over when and how our careers end. Mergers, acquisitions, shifts in management or strategic direction, restructurings, and unexpected personal events may not lead to an immediate exit, but they can set things in motion.

At age fifty-seven, Sally McBride, senior marketing associate at Benson & Sons, loses her job due to a corporate downsizing. Distraught and fearful after learning of her termination, she turns to her friend Thelma Brooks, a retired librarian, for solace and direction. Together, they begin planning, over coffee, the next phase of Sally's life, including creating a realistic vision of retirement.

Included are profound insights and lessons from true stories plus a self-reflective exercise to assist you in envisioning life after work. Two examples of a retirement vision are presented.

"Sally, would you please step into my office?" The request was made by Corey Windermere, the vice-president of marketing for Benson & Sons, Sally's boss. Benson & Sons is a Canadian manufacturer of household appliances.

Sally McBride is a senior marketing associate. She has been with the firm for twenty-seven years. She began as a shipping assistant at the company. Through hard work, dedication, and a cheerful personality, she earned her current position five years ago. As a senior marketing associate, Sally is responsible for client relations within Eastern Canada and the Eastern United States.

Sally is widowed. Pierre, her husband of twenty-eight years, died of a stroke three years ago, leaving her with two sons, Jerry (twenty-four) and Michael (twenty-two), and a daughter, Emily (eighteen). Though she inherited $100,000 plus the ownership of the two-storey home in which she and Pierre had lived for twenty years, Sally continued to work to support herself, her children, and her aged mother. Sally's mother, Agnes, is eighty-seven and has Alzheimer's. She lives in the Three Oaks nursing home, located twenty-five miles from Sally's home.

Prior to today's meeting with Corey Windermere, Sally had planned to continue working at Benson until she was sixty-five.

As Sally walked into Corey's office, she was asked to take a seat. Corey walked around his desk and closed the office door, which was unusual. As the door closed, Sally got a knot in her stomach. Something was wrong. She could feel it.

Corey sat down and said, "Sally, I've some unpleasant news to share with you. Benson & Sons has hit a major financial speed bump. The fire we experienced at our main warehouse last month resulted in the total loss of four months' worth of stock. Though we are scrambling, as you know, to replace the inventory, many of our clients have been switching to other suppliers and may not return to Benson.

"To add to the company's problems, we've been losing

market share to online discount sellers. Further, yesterday we received notice of a twenty percent increase on export duties for all products shipped to the US, our major market.

"Putting all this together, our president has called for drastic cuts in expenditures, including staff reductions. Sally, I'm sorry to say your position as senior marketing associate will be eliminated at the end of the month. I hate telling you this. I know this comes as a shock, and I wish the news was different. Of course, Benson & Sons will provide you with a severance package and will continue your company benefits for six months. I personally will write a glowing reference letter, and if there is anything I can do to help you find another job, please don't hesitate to let me know."

Recently my job was out-sourced and I was terminated. It was a huge shock to me and for several weeks I felt a range of emotions, everything from anger to despair. Then I began to pick up the pieces and never looked back.
— Roger B., consultant

I resigned from the fire department after failing my annual physical. I deeply miss the brother- and sisterhood. It's something knowing you have a group of people you can trust your life to and know they have your back.
— Jack W., newly retired

I loved my job at the post office, but it didn't love me. Bad weather, continual technological changes, and ever-tightening deadlines — I knew it was time to call it quits and retire.
— Peggy S., retiree

Though Corey said positive things about her work performance and dedication to Benson & Sons, his words became a blur. In Sally's mind, questions began quickly surfacing: "Why is this happening to me?" "How will I pay my bills?" "What's going to happen to my children and mother?" "Will I be able to find a new job?" "Who will hire someone who's fifty-seven?" "What am I going to tell my children?" "Am I now facing retirement?"

For what seemed to be an eternity, Sally walked from Corey's office in a daze back to her work area. As she sat, tears began to flow and she sobbed uncontrollably. Margaret, a work colleague, came over and asked what had happened. Sally blurted out she'd just received notice her job is to be eliminated at month's end. Margaret was shocked by the news and tried to console Sally. She asked if Sally had someone she could turn to for comfort and advice. Sally thought of Thelma Brooks, an old friend. Sally thanked Margaret for her concern and reached for her phone to call Thelma.

Thelma is sixty-two and recently retired. Before retiring, she worked as a librarian in a public library. Sally has known Thelma for more than fifteen years. They met at a community reading circle sponsored by Thelma's library. Though not close, Sally and Thelma appreciate each other's sense of thoughtfulness and caring. One of the things Sally likes about Thelma is her positive attitude toward life and her ability to dissect a problem.

"Hi, Thelma, it's Sally. It's been a while since we touched base. I just received news that my job here at Benson is to be eliminated at the end of this month because of company restructuring. Thelma, I'm scared. I thought my job was secure and I'd be working here for another eight years. Getting a similar job in marketing at my age may be impossible. I don't know if I'm looking at retirement, something I didn't think I would be doing at this time in my life. I really need to talk to someone and thought of you. I hope you don't mind me disturbing you. Would you be able to meet me and help with where I go from here?"

Thelma answered, "I'm so sorry. Of course, I'll help anyway I can. Let's meet at Chuck's Café tomorrow at ten. In the meantime, jot down whatever you'd like to talk about."

"Oh thank you, Thelma! I really appreciate it. See you tomorrow."

As Sally hung up the phone, she dried her eyes, took several deep breaths, and tried to settle her nerves. She thought, "What's going to happen to me? How is life going to change? Am I ready for a new life?"

At 10 a.m., Sally arrived at Chuck's, an old Victorian house turned café and bar. It featured a split level that patrons loved for the upper floor's quiet ambient setting and comfy overstuffed chairs. The neighbourhood also made it a sure bet for privacy. Chuck's was particularly popular with coffee connoisseurs.

A few minutes later, Thelma arrived. "Sorry I'm late, Sally. I ran into traffic on my way here from the gym."

As Thelma settled into her chair beside Sally, she said, "Again, I was so sad to learn about you parting ways with Benson. I know you love your job and the people you work with. You must feel shattered. How can I help?"

Sally thanked Thelma for meeting her. "Thelma, last

night, as you suggested, I wrote out some questions. I know there are many others, but right now things look bad. One point that kept going through my mind: I don't think I have enough money to retire. I'm supporting myself, my children, and my mom, you know. I don't think I will ever work in marketing again. Maybe I'll have to sell my house. Thelma, I've never been so scared in my life."

"I want to help you. Now, let's not jump to any conclusions yet. Let's begin by just talking options. Given your twenty-seven years of service with Benson & Sons, what do you think your severance package will be?"

"I don't really know. Why?" Sally asked.

"From my understanding of reading employment law, courts normally consider the person's age, position, length of service, and likelihood of gaining similar employment when determining a satisfactory severance. With your twenty-seven years of service and age, you'll likely receive at least eighteen months of severance pay. Also, you'll be eligible to apply for Employment Insurance. Of course, my advice is to consult with a lawyer specializing in labour law before accepting any severance. And don't walk away without a glowing reference letter."

Sally looked surprised. "Eighteen months of severance. Really, that much! Maybe retirement or semi-retirement is a possibility."

"Okay, let's think about retirement for a moment," said Thelma. "What does the word *retirement* mean to you, Sally?"

After a moment, Sally said, "The first image that comes to mind is being unproductive. A big part of my identity is my job. When I meet someone new and they ask me what

I do, I answer proudly, 'I'm a senior marketing associate with Benson & Sons.' If I'm retired, I think I'd have difficulty changing job titles and calling myself retired."

"Many people see themselves in retirement as being unproductive, contributing nothing, and just heading for death. People who have this pessimistic view end up withdrawing from the world. They don't expect much from retirement, and, unfortunately, that's just what they get.

"But the good news is that it doesn't have to be that way. By adopting a zest for life, no matter their circumstances, people in retirement can be enthusiastic about their futures and shape their destinies.

"So, imagine you are retired. What makes you happy?"

"What will make me happy is being able to pay my bills on time and financially helping my children achieve their dreams," answered Sally. "Also, I'm able to take at least one big trip every few years, and I'm using my work skills that I've acquired throughout my career."

"What skills do you have?" asked Thelma.

"Organizational skills, also my people skills. I seem to be good at goal setting, and I've an ability to consult openly with others. I'm also fairly good at dealing with stressful situations — though my current situation feels outside of my control."

"Is there anything you don't like to do?" asked Thelma.

"Yes," said Sally. "I really don't like being trapped in a job or activity where most of what I do is administrative work. Don't ever put me into an accounting or clerical job. I'd hate it."

"Okay, given what you've told me, describe some activities that would make you happy in retirement."

"Working in marketing, maybe part-time. Possibly working with a start-up firm building their marketing program. Also working or volunteering for a non-profit organization such as the SPCA (Society for the Prevention of Cruelty to Animals).

"You know, Thelma, to be honest, I've never really considered volunteering before. But if I was working with people who have the same interests I have, it may be fun, plus it could give me a routine, something I have at Bensons."

"What else would make you happy in retirement or semi-retirement?" prompted Thelma.

"Well, the time I have with my children — sharing in their lives, providing them with advice and love, and supporting them," said Sally. "And one day, being the best grandmother who walked the earth. Then there is meeting someone who I can share my life with, my Mr. Right, second time around."

"What scares you about retirement?" asked Thelma.

"Not having enough money to finance my dreams," answered Sally. "And, of course, not being physically and mentally healthy to enjoy my retirement years."

"Sally, you're at a stage of life where you need to write a new job description of who you are and who you want to be. It's time to develop and strengthen your ability to find satisfaction in new interests and pursuits. That's not to say you should ignore what you used to do for a living, but it's time to include traveller, volunteer, grandparent, lover, etc., into your description of yourself.

"Remember, make notes of your thoughts, and when we meet in, say, three days, I'd like you to share your vision. Agreed? And don't be surprised if there are some questions you can't answer yet. This is normal when starting out. Also, as I said earlier, I want you to talk to a labour lawyer about your severance package. When I get home, I'll email you three or four names of lawyers I know of. There is one I'd highly recommend. His name is Mark Grier. He's very good."

Successful retirees emphasize the importance of having some sort of written record, including documentation of your retirement plan, actions taken, thoughts, perspectives, and observations. Writing can be an effective way to manage stress and enhance personal growth. It allows you to express your dreams, purpose in life, memories, and feelings.

Sally agreed and said she was looking forward to the next meeting.

I am a nurse about four months from retirement. As I listened to your presentation, I realized I felt extremely depressed because I, too, equated retirement with the end of "usefulness." Luckily, the message that retirement didn't have to be that way has sunk in. I am ready to create my own "useful" next phase. I know this sounds like an exaggeration, but it's entirely sincere. You saved my life!
— Wilma F., retired nurse

Many people retire from work they did not enjoy; however, their former role can still create problems.

My husband did not enjoy his work, but when he retired, he

seemed to apply his former role of manager to me. This created arguments that ended with me begging him to find something to get him out of the house. It wasn't until he angrily pointed out I kept referring to the house as "my" house that I realized I needed to make some adjustments, too.
— Rita A., homemaker

A successful retirement includes focusing on what you do now, not just on what you used to do. Thinking of yourself as a retired supervisor, manager, professor, or nurse — or just plain retired — is limiting.

It has been said that the life we lead is a result of the choices we make. In your pre-retirement and retirement years, it's important for you to make the right choices — the ones that will result in building a fulfilling and energetic retirement. Visualization helps you create a mental model of retirement and helps to prepare you for making the right choices.

Frances, a busy sixty-three-year-old supervisor, is employed at a major manufacturing company. Through the years she contributed to her Registered Retirement Saving Plan (RRSP), though retirement wasn't part of her everyday thinking. It was just something that would happen down the road.

When Frances actually began thinking about retirement, she was at a loss as to what to do with the rest of her life. She didn't have a hobby, didn't like to exercise, hadn't volunteered, and had no interests outside of her work and family. For Frances, retirement appeared bleak and unappealing.

After receiving advice from a retired friend, Frances began to visualize what she wanted from retirement. She imagined herself as an above-average tennis player (she played tennis in her twenties); she saw herself being fit and exercising regularly (she used to jog three times a week until ten years ago); she visualized herself doing some type of volunteer activity and giving back to her community. Frances began taking the first steps to building her retirement future.

The goal you set must be challenging. At the same time, it should be realistic and attainable, not impossible to reach. It should be challenging enough to make you stretch, but not so far that you break.
— Rick Hansen

I envision myself continuing in my profession but only working two days a week. My wife and I are having fun together, attending auctions, attending concerts, and travelling. I am spending about one day a week doing volunteer work. I see myself curling twice a week in the winter and golfing once a week during the spring and summer. I am eating healthy meals and exercising regularly. I envision my wife and I spending about twenty percent of our time with our children and grandchildren.
—Bill F., plumber

The quality of your retirement is up to you. Once you have created your vision, share it with your spouse or partner and close friends. Explain to them, in as much detail as possible, what you're doing in retirement (e.g., continuing in your profession or trade), the new activities you are attempting, who you have as a support system, where you want to be living, your health and diet, and all other aspects of who you are and where you want to be.

As you describe your vision, make note of what questions come to mind and those asked of you. Fill in the grey areas. Ask for suggestions on how you can achieve your retirement goals. Brainstorm ideas and solutions with those closest to you and record the findings. Take time to consider the input. Which suggestions make sense to you and which ones are unrealistic? Review your written vision and make changes as necessary. At the end of this process, you should have a clear picture of your retirement life. It is true that the visualization process and drafting of a balanced retirement plan takes time and effort, but it is worthwhile. A well-thought-out retirement vision acts as your anchor and your compass for direction and future decisions.

EXERCISE 1

Take a few minutes to relax and visualize what the word *retirement* means to you. What is it about retirement that attracts, scares, or excites you?

_____

_____

_____

_____

_____

_____

_____

_____

Try to visualize as much detail as possible. Don't be discouraged if your picture is fuzzy and lacking in detail. Clarity is close at hand.

In my retirement:

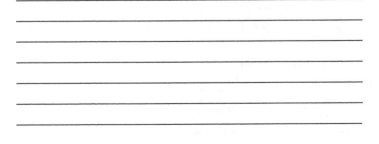

Now imagine yourself specifically in your first six months of retirement. Then in one and two years. Does your mental picture change? If so, how? Take a moment to record your thoughts.

I'm imagining I've been retired for:

Six months

_____

_____

_____

_____

_____

_____

_____

_____

Twelve months

_____

_____

_____

_____

_____

_____

_____

Twenty-four months

_____

_____

_____

_____

_____

_____

_____

_____

Now visualize yourself at the end of your retirement when you're ninety, ninety-five, or over a hundred. What are you most proud of? What have you done that brought happiness to you and others? What will you be remembered for?

_____

_____

_____

_____

_____

_____

_____

_____

Think about the people you know who have made a success of their retirement. What do they do that you admire? Is it their family relationships, their energy and enthusiasm, or perhaps their sense of well-being? Take a moment to record your observations.

_____

_____

_____

_____

_____

_____

_____

Now think of those who are challenged by retirement. What are they doing or not doing that makes them, in your opinion, less successful in retirement? Is it the abnormal amount of time they spend watching television, their lack of adventure, or their possible sense of helplessness in an ever-changing world?

_____

_____

_____

_____

_____

_____

_____

_____

Chapter 2

Getting Ready to Make the Plunge

Summary:

According to a 2017 study completed by the Transamerica Center for Retirement Studies and Instituto de Longevidade Mongeral Aegon, one in five people in the world can expect to live beyond their ninetieth birthday. The study found that those who are in good health and stay socially connected have a more positive outlook about their future, which leads to a greater probability of achieving retirement success.

Sally is introduced to Rique Rousseau. He worked as an executive and retired fourteen years ago. Rique is a friend of Thelma's, and together Rique and Sally explore the importance of creating a balanced leisure lifestyle. Rique shares his lifestyle activities relating to entertainment, education, travel, sports, social activities, and hobbies.

This chapter will also cover listing additional lifestyle activities, the dangers of procrastination, advice to couples when establishing a leisure lifestyle, and a true-life story about exercise routines.

At the end of the chapter are five exercises. They address the following: identifying personal needs, prioritizing your needs, how best to meet personal needs, comparing retirement visions — original to current, and additions/deletions to your plans.

As arranged, Sally and Thelma met again at Chuck's Café to continue their conversation on retirement planning. Over the previous three days, Sally thought a lot about what retirement would look like.

Sally had written down what she thought her retirement should be like:

I envision myself continuing in my marketing profession but working only two days a week. I'm having fun with my children. I'm spending one day a week doing volunteer work, teaching small children how to read, or working with animals. I'd like to be in better shape and, hopefully, meet a new life partner.

When Thelma entered Chuck's Café, she had with her an older gentleman named Rique Rousseau, a former vice-president for Tridon Electronics in Montreal, Quebec. Rique was tall, tanned, and robust. He had a calming way about him.

"Hi, Sally, good to see you again," said Thelma. "I brought Rique Rousseau with me. Rique is a friend of my family whom I've known for many years. I may have mentioned him. He lives in Montreal and is in town for a couple of days working on a project with his volunteer organization, the Canadian Executive Service Organization. I told him about your possible retirement because I thought he may be able to offer some useful ideas. I hope you don't mind me inviting him."

"No, I welcome all the help I can get," said Sally. "Rique, how long have you been retired?"

"Fourteen years now. Before retiring, I was a vice-president for Tridon Electronics. My job involved project management and a lot of travelling around the world. To be honest, the pace was making me tired, which meant I didn't pay attention to my marriage and children. After a health scare, I decided I'd had enough and retired on my sixty-third birthday. Best decision I ever made. I didn't realize how stressed I was working and being on call twenty-four seven. Thelma shared a little of your background, and you're considering retirement. Am I right?"

"Yes, my job at Benson & Sons is being eliminated, and Thelma is helping me figure out what comes next. At our last meeting, she asked me to envision my retirement. I was concerned about what I'm going to do with my time. I'm thinking of working part-time and volunteering. Also, I want to get into better shape through exercise and eating well. I know I should be more specific with my wants and needs, but at this time my thinking is a bit erratic. But what would I do with my spare time?"

"Sally, that is one of the key issues separating unsuccessful retirees and successful retirees — what to do with leisure time," said Rique. "When I stopped working, I saw slowing down, relaxing, and playing as my rewards for all my years of hard work. It was like entering vacation mode. It felt great for a couple of weeks and then I began getting bored — watching TV for hours and hours. I turned my attention to playing golf, a game I played once a month when working. After retiring, I was playing six days a week, and I began to hate the game."

Rique continued, "I then read *Don't Just Retire — Live It, Love It!* and *Strategies for Retiring Right!* written by

Rick Atkinson. In his books, Rick outlines the need to step back and identify one's personal needs and ask if it's enough to be included in one's retirement planning. For me, I identified five personal needs: challenge, family, health, pleasure, and service.

"When I was creating my retirement plan, I built in actions that help meet my needs. For instance, with my challenge needs, I assess potential projects and activities from the point of view of being interesting and thought-provoking. Currently, I'm the assistant director of theatre at a local high school. Not only does this provide a challenge, it also fulfills my service needs. As part of my family needs, I'm reconnecting with my cousins, nieces, and nephews. My health and pleasure needs are part of my balanced leisure lifestyle, something I learned about when reading Rick's books."

"What is a balanced leisure lifestyle and how do you create one?" asked Sally.

"Many retirees have largely unstructured days, and that has a negative effect. They end up in a state of malaise. Rick recommends building a balanced leisure lifestyle, one that has at least one regular activity in six different categories: entertainment, education, travel, exercise, social activities, and hobbies.

"With entertainment, I do things that both stimulate my mind and provide healthy diversions and amusement," Rique continued. "My wife and I enjoy foreign films and off-Broadway plays. We both watch *Coronation Street* and *Saturday Night Live*. I like to go to baseball games and poke around antique shops. My wife and I have regular date nights; sometimes we go out for special dinners or just take simple walks in the park.

"With education, I'm learning to speak Spanish. I joined Ancestry.com to learn more about my family roots, and once every two weeks I take cooking classes for men who have never cooked.

"As far as travel is concerned, when I was working, I visited many countries around the world, and my wife often joined me. When we discussed travel during retirement, we settled on exploring out-of-the-way places such as Mongolia, Canada's Arctic, and North Africa. We stay at B&Bs and hostels to help us get to know the locals. We also stay in one place for at least a week to experience the community life.

"For my exercise routine, I bike for thirty minutes every second day and power-walk when its not raining. On inclement days, I practice yoga. Before I started exercising, I asked my doctor for a complete physical. Then I shared my physical exam results with a professional trainer who built a custom program for me. One of my targets is to lose twenty pounds in the next six months and to train for a half-marathon next year.

"Socializing with others is so important when you're retired. For years, many of my social needs were met by the people I worked with and clients I got to know. Of course, when you leave the job, you lose most of these friendships. Most people don't realize the extent to which co-workers help fill the basic need for socialization — the lunchtime talks, coffee breaks, company and industry events. As a result, retirees often find themselves feeling lonely without knowing why.

"I joined Probus, a social organization for people fifty-five years old or older who are semi-retired or retired. I'm out there socializing, meeting people, and making new friends as much as possible. As a result, I can be busy every day if I wanted. My wife too has broadened her social circle to the point where we feel we need appointments to see each other.

"As for hobbies, this was another challenge. Throughout my life, I really didn't have any hobbies. My work was my hobby. I had to go searching. I tried oil painting, woodworking, photography, and making wine and even had a crack at restoring an old Model T Ford. To tell the truth, none of what I tried excited me. Thank goodness I didn't buy a lot of equipment. I borrowed a friend's camera and worked on a buddy's Model T. You know what I found out? I love to cook, much to the delight of my wife.

"Sally, finding your balanced leisure lifestyle will take time, as it did for me. You should experiment with different activities until you find the right mix. Make adjustments over time, too, as the opportunities and your interests change. You might also need adjustments as your physical or financial situations change. The greatest difficulty, I found, to creating a balanced leisure life is procrastination. Try putting notes into your calendar three months, six months, nine months, and one year after your retirement starts. Each note should read, 'Am I living a balanced and satisfactory life?' If not, create a plan for a successful retirement now.' Lastly, don't put off your search; start checking out the fun stuff and get building your leisure plan today.

"Thanks for listening to me, Sally," Rique added. "Unfortunately, I have to run, as my wife and I are scheduled to watch our granddaughter's ballet recital this afternoon. Here is my card. Please call me anytime. I'd be delighted to share my experience in transitioning from work to life after work. Thanks, Thelma, for introducing me to Sally. See you."

Rique gathered up his coat and hat and waved goodbye.

Sally turned to Thelma. "He's an interesting person, and I appreciate him sharing his balanced leisure lifestyle with me. What he has created has got me thinking about my own leisure lifestyle. I'm excited to begin my search. However, there is one area I'm concerned about and that is how work and volunteering would fit into my lifestyle."

"At our next meeting, I'd like to introduce you to Shivani and Gomad Kaur," said Thelma. "They are about your age and have two children, one of whom suffers from multiple sclerosis. Both Shivani and Gomad have been retired for two years. Due to a limited income and their adult daughter's illness, they both work part-time and volunteer. I think you will be inspired by how they not only created a balanced leisure lifestyle but also included work and volunteering into their retirement lives."

"Sounds good. I'm look forward to meeting them. In the meantime, I've got some thinking to do about my balanced leisure lifestyle. Rique helped fill in several grey areas, especially around the entertainment and socializing I may include in my plan."

"Are you available early next week, say, Monday? I'll check with Shivani and Gomad to see if they are free."

"Yes, Monday works for me." Sally entered the date into her iPhone calendar.

On the drive home, Sally thought about both her leisure

lifestyle and the money needed to fund her plans. When she thought about each of the lifestyle segments (entertainment, education, travel, exercise, social activities, and hobbies), the following activities flashed into her mind:

- Entertainment: Watching my favourite shows on TV (*The View*, 10 p.m. News, *60 Minutes*). Taking in stage plays presented by a local theatrical group. Hosting dinner parties and get-togethers with friends.
- Education: Learning French and researching my family through genealogical websites. I'd like to create a family tree, as my children may appreciate learning more about their heritage.
- Travel: Though I enjoy travelling, being single makes it more difficult due to the premiums travel companies often charge. Then there is the thought of eating alone. I have to do more research in this area. I'll call Trafalgar and ask for information about tours for singles.
- Exercise: This is another area needing attention. I should build an exercise program. Maybe I'll take Rique's suggestion and hire a personal trainer to help with my regime.
- Social activities: Though I attend church (not as frequently as I could), I don't take the time to participate in the after-service coffee klatches held in the church basement. I should make time to introduce myself to fellow parishioners — you never know, I may meet new friends: mmmm … could Mr. Right be one of them? I do have coffee with my girlfriends from college, though these gathering are becoming more infrequent. When I think about it, many of my social

relationships are bound in some way with Benson. Maybe I'll check out Probus and attend one or two local meetings.

- Hobbies: I've tried hobbies. Let's see, there was flower arranging, scrapbooking, jewelry making, and knitting. None held my interest for more than a month or so. Finding a hobby or two should be on my "get to it" list.

Maybe Shivani and Gomad would have other ideas about how best to create a balanced leisure lifestyle. If stuck, Sally could call Rique and, of course, talk to Thelma. With all these resources, plus her girlfriends, Sally wasn't worried about creating her lifestyle. However, the one thought that concerned her was how to fit work into her plan.

Additional Balanced Leisure Lifestyle Suggested Activities

Entertainment: Reading, watching your favourite television shows, dining out, attending symphonies, operas, concerts, movies, and/or ballgames.

Education: Learning a new language or a new craft, becoming an expert in financial planning, becoming a history buff, studying genealogy.

Travel: Cruising, long road trips, camping, visiting out-of-town friends for a few days, participating in tour company travel packages.

Sports: Hiking, biking, golf, swimming, fishing, playing tennis, power walking, lawn bowling, skiing, ice fishing. Retirees should have at least one sport component in their leisure plan.

Social activities: Service clubs (e.g., Lions, Rotary, etc.), interest groups, social clubs, visiting with relatives, playing bingo. Anything that gets you out of the house and into a social setting participating with others.

Hobbies: Genealogy, oil painting, folk art, antique collecting, trout fly tying, gourmet cooking, gardening, model building, photography, stamp or coin collecting, furniture refinishing, sculpture, needlepoint, flower arranging, wine tasting, car restoring, woodworking, paper tole, to name a few.

Finding the right combination of entertainment, education, travel, sports, social activities, and hobbies to match your lifestyle and personality takes time and effort.

Experiment and Adjust Over Time

My knees became so bad I could barely walk up and down stairs. Though I knew going to the pool for water exercises would help, the thought of dealing with the ladder was too much, and I stopped going. Two weeks later, a friend from class called to see if I was okay. After hemming and hawing over the reason for my absence, I finally confessed. To my surprise, she laughed and then reminded me she uses the lift to get into and out of the pool. I went back the next week and only suffered from being teased.
— Norma E., artist

Procrastination stops you before you even get started.

The greatest impediment to creating a balanced leisure

lifestyle is procrastination. We sometimes tell ourselves, "I'll start my search next month," but then this elusive "next month" never comes.

Some retirees find that such procrastination eventually becomes unhealthy. They describe becoming gradually disenchanted with retirement. Some even sink deeply into isolation and develop a habit of low expectations. To avoid these problems, I recommend using a calendar to set review points.

Balance for Couples

Couples occasionally try to establish a leisure lifestyle in which they do everything together. Although this works for some couples, most couples find it impossible to achieve in a healthy way. There is good reason for that: Being a couple doesn't mean both people have identical interests and needs.

Just as everyone should experiment to find the right mix of activities, couples should experiment to find the right balance of things they do together and things they do separately. It's also important for couples to communicate about this. Discuss expectations, any feelings of exclusion, and budget issues.

EXERCISE 2 — PART ONE

Review each of the following common needs and ask if it is important enough to be included in your retirement planning. If so, circle it and proceed to Part Two.

Achievement: Accomplishing tasks, being the best

Affection: Giving and receiving kindness, companionship

Affiliation: Being accepted, feeling a sense of belonging

Autonomy: Being your own person, establishing priorities and time schedules

Challenge: Getting involved in interesting and thought-provoking endeavours

Competence: Being respected and recognized for skills and abilities

Expertise: Becoming a respected authority in something

Family: Having time and meaningful relationships with loved ones

Growth: Challenging yourself to be constantly learning and reaching your full potential

Health: Being physically and mentally fit

Integrity: Being honest, true, and conscious of yourself

Leadership: Being able to willfully and responsibly direct and influence the effort of others

Location:	Enjoying your current address, city, region, and country
Money:	Being financially secure
Pleasure:	Enjoying life, having fun
Recognition:	Attaining status, being respected
Security:	Leading a dependable and stable life
Service:	Helping others, contributing to their well-being
Spirituality:	Possessing inner harmony and peace, living by beliefs

Add other personal needs not listed:

_____

_____

_____

_____

_____

_____

_____

_____

PART TWO

Now it's time to prioritize your list of needs. What need is most important to you? Which one ranks second? Prioritize your list below.

Need #1 _____

Need #2 _____

Need #3 _____

Need #4 _____

Need #5 _____

Need #6 _____

Need #7 _____

Need #8 _____

PART THREE

Visualize a retirement that meets your top six prioritized needs. Creating a vision with more than six needs is difficult and can be frustrating. In your retirement vision, what are you doing, who are you with, what leisure activities are you participating in, and what makes up your typical day, what is your diet like, and what is your state of mind? Write your vision below.

_____

_____

_____

_____

_____

_____

_____

_____

PART FOUR

Compare your retirement vision with your original retirement picture outlined in Exercise 1. Based on your prioritized needs, what changes are necessary? What additions or deletions to your original picture are required? Write them below.

_____

_____

_____

_____

_____

_____

_____

Your vision of retirement should satisfy your personal wants and needs. If your retirement vision does not reflect what's important to you, your retirement plans will be out of balance and they won't feel right.

If you identify health and fitness as a highly important need, you must include appropriate measures to ensure that need is met in your plan. Actions designed to achieve a healthy lifestyle may include changing your diet, engaging in regular exercise, and using meditation techniques. Being healthy doesn't just happen — it takes work.

If you have a need for stability and security, placing

your retirement nest egg into risky financial ventures may result in sleepless nights and worry. Investing in more stable financial instruments such as guaranteed investment certificates (GICs), bonds, and mutual funds may give you a greater sense of security. Continuing to work in some capacity may also contribute to your need for stability.

Throughout the retirement visioning process, it is imperative to be optimistic about your future. Focus on the rewards of a balanced retirement. Enjoy feeling complete, being enriched and financially secure. Review and rewrite your retirement vision as often as required until it feels right and is in line with your wants, needs, and beliefs.

When you have drafted your retirement vision, ask yourself the following questions:

1. Is my vision clear and understandable?   Yes / No
Remember, it's okay to have undefined parts of your retirement vision. These are just areas you have to think about further.

2. Is my vision brief but comprehensive?   Yes / No
Over time, your retirement vision will crystallize and be your guide.

3. Does my vision have a primary focus?   Yes / No
Having a vision concentrated on meeting four to six important personal needs will be more manageable and achievable than if you tried to meet eight or nine needs.

4. Is my vision flexible enough to change?   Yes / No
Recognize that your personal needs today may not be the

same a few years from now. Down the road, you may require additional medical assistance and increased family support.

5. Does my vision serve as a guide that will help me make good decisions? **Yes / No**

6. Does my vision reflect my values, beliefs and philosophy? **Yes / No**

7. Is my vision representative of who I am? **Yes / No**

8. Is my vision attainable? **Yes / No**
If you build an unrealistic retirement vision, you may set yourself up for failure.

9. Does my vision inspire me? **Yes /No**
When you read and think about your vision, does it excite and give you positive feelings?

EXERCISE 3

As stated previously, the quality of your vision and your retirement is up to you. Share your vision with your spouse or partner and close friends.

Based on the comments and suggestions of others, what additions or deletions will you make to your retirement vision?

_____

_____

_____

_____

_____

_____

_____

_____

Chapter 3

Working and Volunteering
As Part of Your Lifestyle

Summary:

Working

For some, the thought of working in retirement is foreign and they outright reject the idea. For others, especially those who may not have sufficient savings or who love to work, being gainfully employed after retirement is quite attractive. For these people, paid work represents an acknowledgement of their self-worth and contributions, while for others, it is an opportunity to have new colleagues and workmates.

Volunteering

Many retirees tell me the one thing they miss most from their working lives is the structure. It's the need to get up in the morning, be at work for a certain time, attend meetings, solve problems, be with people, and have a sense of accomplishment. As a volunteer, you are able to give back through your time and talents, to the benefit of others. It can be a fulfilling way to be involved and get the structure you are looking for.

In this chapter, we will meet Silvani and Gomad. They both volunteer and work part-time out of necessity to pay for their daughter's health expenses. As friends of Thelma, they outline to Sally the benefits of volunteering and counsel her in how to say no when a volunteer agency wants more of your time.

Later in this chapter are two exercises. The first one will help you determine if a paying job or starting a business should be part of your retirement plan. The second one will help you identify your volunteering interests.

On Monday, Sally made her way to Chuck's Café to meet Silvani and Gomad. When she arrived, Thelma, Silvani, and Gomad were already seated and enjoying their lattes. Thelma introduced everyone. They shook hands, and for the next few minutes the conversation was about Chuck's, the weather, and the neighbourhood.

Thelma then opened the topic of creating a balanced leisure lifestyle and how to blend it with working and volunteering.

"When Gomad and I were raising our family," Silvani said, "we knew retirement would be challenging. I met Gomad when I was working in a print shop. He was the salesperson for a paper company, and our shop was one of his clients. Within six months, we were married, and two years later, our first daughter, Lisa, was born. Angela, our second, arrived twelve months after Lisa. We were devastated when we learned Angela had multiple sclerosis. Throughout our married life, money was a continual topic of conversation, as Angela's care is expensive, even with medicare."

Silvani continued, "Each month was a challenge paying our bills and trying to invest for the future. In the end, we saved a little over $150,000 for retirement. Two years ago, Angela's condition worsened, which we knew would happen as she grew older. Because of that, I took early retirement. At about the same time, Gomad's paper supply firm was bought out by a large European company. Since Gomad was sixty-five, he decided to take a severance package and leave to better support Angela and me."

"The issue we faced prior to retiring was the need to work," said Gomad. "Keeping in mind Angela's schedule and expenses, I work part-time as a night supervisor for a shipping company and Silvani works every second day for a florist."

In today's employment environment, there is a demand for older workers. Companies are willing to hire older people, as it often means spending less time, energy, and money on orientation and training of new employees. Many employers view retirees as steady and more reliable than younger workers, and older workers require less time off. Retirees traditionally have a strong work ethic and are often able to work flexible hours during the day. This makes them a good source of people power for relief work on weekends and for vacations and sick time.

"One of the benefits of paid jobs, over and above the money, is the appreciation of our leisure time," Gomad said. "Of course, there is a greater need to plan and manage our leisure time. During the week, with the help of a home care provider, Silvani and I have one evening together that we use to take ballroom dancing classes. We even dance around the house. Angela loves when we dance. She beats time to the music on her wheelchair."

"Also, part of our retirement includes volunteering with the Multiple Sclerosis Society of Canada," said Silvani.

"Over the years, Gomad and I have learned so much about MS and patient care that we want to give back and help others. We get so much gratification in seeing other parents with MS children develop and succeed. We have a tremendous sense of pride, while at the same time earning the respect of others. And we have met many new people with similar interests, challenges, and perspectives. Not only do we receive thank-yous from those we help; the MS Society has published notes of recognition of our service in their newsletter and has honoured us on special occasions."

The options for volunteering are limitless. Examples of volunteer activities include the following:

- Teaching English as a second language
- Assisting new immigrant children with math and other school subjects
- Assisting in local art galleries, museums, and zoos
- Volunteering in local hospitals
- Working with disadvantaged youth
- Delivering meals to shut-ins
- Counselling young mothers
- Participating in housing programs such as Habitat for Humanity

"One word of caution about working or volunteering. Don't be lulled into thinking it will generate enough money for a successful retirement. It won't. We've found working for a paycheque and volunteering are only part of our retirement. We still need to concentrate on actively planning and managing our leisure time. Every few months we remind ourselves of our commitment to have fun, keep learning, take side trips, ensure we're exercising, keep meeting people, and pursue our hobbies. For me, my hobby is pen and ink drawing. Gomad's is photography."

After listening to Silvani and Gomad, Sally said, "Thank you so much for sharing with me. The two of you are an inspiration, and you've given me a lot to think about. I have a couple of questions for you, if you don't mind."

"Of course not," said Gomad.

"Like you, I feel I need money. My retirement savings and pension will not be enough. But what is enough?"

"Often we're told we need $500,000 or $1 million to retire on," Silvani said. "Ask a person with $500,000 in retirement savings how much they need for retirement, and they will probably say they need more than what they have. Ask a person with $1 million or $3 million, and the answer will be the same. In my mind, the monetary trick to a happy retirement is not to concentrate on amassing an abnormal amount of wealth but to determine how much money will make you feel secure. In other words, how much money do you need to enable youself to live and fulfill your visualized retirement lifestyle?"

"In a practical sense, how you spend your retirement time determines how much money you will need," Gomad said. "If you plan to travel the world or indulge in expensive hobbies such as sailing, your financial needs will be much greater than those of someone with more modest plans. What you don't want is to envision a retirement you can't afford. All this does is cause anxiety and unease. By creating a retirement that is realistic and affordable, you gain satisfaction and peace of mind. Financially estimating your retirement plans is the key to determining the amount of money required."

"Thank you both for your insight," Sally said. "My other question is how do I say no when I'm volunteering?"

Silvani laughed. "I've heard this question many times from both volunteers and those interested in volunteering. When considering volunteering, ask yourself: How much time do I want to commit? Is the answer three hours a day, one morning a week, or two days a week? Once you decide what makes sense to you, stick to your time allocation until you're sure you can and want to handle more. You'll also need to learn to say no because volunteer organizations are constantly looking for additional help. It's easy to find yourself bombarded with requests, and you can become overwhelmed. Don't be afraid to say, 'Thanks but no thanks.' And if the hours become too much and you're no longer happy with the arrangement, you might have to quit."

Sally said, "Again, thank you for your time. I really appreciate meeting you, and thanks, Thelma, for introducing me to Silvani and Gomad. I do hope we stay in contact."

EXERCISE 4

Answer the following questions based on your personal needs. If you have six or more "yes" answers, you should consider either a paying job or starting a business as part of your retirement plan.

	Yes	No
I have a strong work ethic that needs to be satisfied	___	___
I need to feel I've accomplished something each day; only a paying job will fulfill my need	___	___
Working for money is important to me	___	___
I need a paying job to wake up to	___	___
Work keeps me in the mainstream and in contact with others in my profession or trade	___	___
Work keeps my mind active	___	___
I need the money	___	___
Working part-time will help me enjoy my leisure time more	___	___
Work is pleasure for me — as long as I get paid for it	___	___
Work is therapeutic; it will keep me alive longer	___	___
Total Score	___	___

As a second option, you may be interested in starting your own business in any one discipline such as consulting, home decorating, small engine repair, tax form completion, senior care, child care, furniture restoration, dog walking, tutoring, cake decorating, caretaking, organizational coach, garage sale convener, hairstyling, pet sitting, bicycle repair, or even wedding or event planning.

List three or four work choices that interest you:

_____

_____

_____

_____

_____

_____

_____

_____

EXERCISE 5

List the organizations or activities you would be interested in volunteering for. Select one or two you plan to explore regarding volunteer opportunities.

Organizations/activities that interest me	Action plan
e.g., my place of worship	In the next week, I will contact my religious leader about volunteering.

_____

_____

_____

_____

_____

_____

_____

April was a nurse in a busy city hospital. When she retired, she took time off to simply unwind and relax. After a couple of months, she felt the urge to return to nursing and she approached her previous employer about working part-time. Her employer jumped at the chance, and now April works two night shifts per week.

April's part-time nursing job provides her with additional income, plus her work schedule permits time for her to enjoy both her leisure and volunteer activities. She volunteers with Meals on Wheels and is an instructor with St. John Ambulance.

Getting involved in helping others through volunteering or advocacy work has a great effect on mental health. There's nothing better for your brain than trying to help someone else.

— William Shatner

Chapter 4

The Straight Goods on Money

Summary:

In the years leading up to the financial crisis of 2007 and 2008, sometimes referred to as the "lost decade," job growth was stagnant and the stock market recorded its worst ten-year performance in history. For many fiftysomethings, these years meant their investments weren't growing and neither were their incomes. Depending on where people had their money invested, some saw more than forty percent of their retirement savings wiped out.

The successful investor is an educated investor. In this chapter, Sally learns the questions to ask when searching for a competent financial service provider. She meets Daniel, a financial advisor, who lays out what he does for his clients.

There is also a case study in which we will look at a couple's experience with their financial advisor.

And there are two exercises. The first one will show you how to calculate your net worth. The second will show you how to prepare a cash flow statement.

"It was so good of Silvani and Gomad to meet with me," said Sally. "What they said has inspired me to find a part-time job I'd like and to, in some way, give back to my community."

"That's great," Thelma said. "Now, let's talk about your

concern about money. When thinking about your life after Benson & Sons, what additional monies do you feel you'll need on a monthly basis?"

After thinking for a moment, Sally answered, "Given my initial plan to stay in my home, the money I may get as part of a severance from Bensons, my personal savings and possibly drawing on my company pension and government pension when I hit age sixty-two, I'm guessing $2,000 per month from part-time work would be enough. That is, if my investments hold steady or, hopefully, rise. But to be honest, I need to take a close look at my savings and pension benefits. With the help of a financial planner, I should be able to estimate how much money I need to retire."

"Tell me about your financial advisor. How did you meet? What is his experience? What types of investments has he recommended? What rates of return are you receiving?"

"Pierre and I met Howard at a Christmas party. I had mentioned to our host that we were in the market for a financial advisor and she introduced us to him. He seemed like a nice guy. A week later, Pierre and I were in his office outlining our financial affairs. Howard did an analysis of our investments and made several recommendations, and I've worked with him ever since."

"Like most Canadians, Pierre and I contributed to our Registered Retirement Savings Plans (RRSPs), and we bought the occasional Canada Savings Bond or whatever investment our advisor recommended. We had no idea what kind of investment return our savings had delivered over the years. I wasn't even sure why we had purchased many of the investments we owned. But when Pierre died, I started to do a little digging and found out our funds were the best investments for our advisor, not necessarily for us. The companies selling these funds provided the best sales commissions and ongoing fees to advisors.

"Though I've been uneasy with my advisor and haven't answered many of his calls, I know I need to work with someone who will put me and my family ahead of his own interest. In preparation for finding a new advisor, I've been reading the business session of the newspaper and searching for investing magazines. I also tune into a local business television show and surf the Internet in search of the latest financial news and views. I don't want someone else in control of my money, but I need to find a financial advisor I can trust."

"Educating yourself is great," said Thelma. "Even if you rely on the recommendations of a financial advisor, you need enough knowledge to be able to evaluate the recommendations to make sure they are in your best interest.

"Three years ago, I was looking for a trustworthy financial advisor. Like you, I began to do my homework and read Gail Beebe's book *No Hype: The Straight Goods on Investing Your Money*. In her book, Gail lists questions to ask a potential financial advisor."

Questions from Gail Bebee's *No Hype: The Straight Goods on Investing Your Money*:

- What are your qualifications?
- How long have you been a financial advisor?
- Who else is on your team?

- How long has your firm been in business?
- Does your firm sell investments as well as provide advice?
- What is your investment philosophy?
- Do you personally buy and sell financial products for clients?
- Do you prepare an investment plan for each of your clients?
- How often will we talk and/or meet?
- How quickly will you respond if I call or email you?
- How are you paid?
- What research, newsletters, etc., do you and your firm provide to clients?
- What kind of account statements do you provide and how frequently?
- Do you provide statements with the original cost, current market value, and return rate of each investment?
- What is your firm's procedure for handling client complaints?

"Gail recommends you develop a short list of potential advisors using family members, friends, and business associates," Thelma continued. "Then interview each one before choosing one. After six months with the new advisor, review the advisor's performance and decide if they have met your expectations. If not, consider hiring the advisor who came second on your original list. When we next meet, I'll bring my copy of Gail's book for you to borrow."

"That would be wonderful! I look forward to reading it," Sally replied.

"Sally, regardless of whether you are working with a financial advisor or handling your money yourself, it's important to match your retirement vision with your money."

The Importance of Budgeting

No matter where you're living or what you plan to do in retirement, you probably want at the very least to maintain your present standard of living. To assist you in this process, personal budgeting is critical. Budgeting helps you determine where your money comes from, where it goes, and how much is left over at the end of the month. It provides you with a clear picture of what your current lifestyle is costing you and your spouse on a monthly basis.

If you're married and only one person has been controlling the family expenses, it's time to change your system. Couples should work out cash plans together. Be sure to include all possible income and determine a realistic estimate of your combined expenses. The more you communicate and work together now, the less likely you are to have costly surprises later on!

"I believe we've had a productive morning," said Thelma. "I'm glad you met Silvani and Gomad and chatted about finding a financial advisor. Would you like to meet my financial advisor, Daniel Thornhill? Knowing you and your needs, it may be a good fit. Daniel's an independent financial advisor I've used for the last five years.

"I believe he is different than most advisors in that he works with clients holistically. What I mean by that is he listens to how you see yourself in retirement and what your future goals and spending patterns will likely be and he builds a financial strategy to help make it all happen.

"Daniel will also take the time to educate you about the world of finance. For instance, when I first began working with him, I told him about the retirement lifestyle I wanted, and together we built a portfolio that would produce the money to make my plans happen. He was honest with me when my plans were bigger than my pocketbook. Maybe you'd like to include him on your list of possible advisors."

"Daniel sounds great. When can I meet him?" asked Sally. "With my current financial advisor, I get the feeling he's only interested in the money aspect of my retirement. I once raised a concern that I may be bored and frustrated if I was retired and I wasn't working. My advisor didn't even acknowledge my concern and immediately switched the conversation to my RRSP. I never even mentioned the stuff that scares me, such as living alone, making new friends, and the relationships with my friends and family."

"Do you have some time right now?" Thelma asked. "Daniel's office is only a couple of blocks from here. I can give him a call and see if he is free."

"Hey, that would be great if we could meet today. I'm really excited to share my retirement vision with him and get his thoughts on how much money I will need."

Thelma called Daniel and, after a couple of minutes, signalled with a thumbs up on his availability.

As Sally and Thelma were walking out of Chuck's, Sally said, "Yesterday I met with Mark Grier, the labour lawyer you mentioned. He was very pleasant. He wanted to know how long I worked at Benson & Sons, my job's duties and responsibilities, the benefits I'm receiving now, and whether I'd accept a lump-sum severance payment or regular pay over a period of time.

"He warned me not to accept a severance package from Benson without him reviewing it. After his review, he will make recommendations for changes based on recent court findings concerning severance and communicate with Benson & Sons, in writing, on my behalf. After my meeting with him, I'm feeling more confident and in control. Thanks for pointing me in his direction."

As they entered Daniel Thornhill's office, Sally noticed the initials CFP on his nameplate. Daniel was a man in his mid-forties. He greeted them.

"Hi, Thelma, great to see you again. And that reminds me. I've got the financial prospectus you were asking for. And you must be Sally!"

Sally shook Daniel's hand, a strong, confident handshake.

"Please, ladies, take a seat and make yourselves comfortable. Sally, I understand you're looking for a new financial advisor. Am I right?"

"Yes, and Thelma had many good things to say about the service you provide."

"I try my best for my clients. My job is to help my clients succeed in retirement not only financially, but also holistically, as I hope Thelma attests to. Pension plans, RRSPs, estate plans are one side of retirement. These topics are common, but I believe today's wealth managers and financial advisors need to offer clients a more holistic approach to retirement, one that encourages exploration and direction beyond money-related questions. Besides money issues, I assist my clients by first listening to their retirement plans, offer comments and observations and blend in discussions on money."

"I can attest to what Daniel said," Thelma said. "More often than not, we discuss family and the future. Some years ago, Daniel and I built a financial plan that encompassed my interests and lifestyle. He works with me to secure my retirement in its totality."

"Sally, I'm not a retirement guru, but I'm aware of all the issues surrounding retirement," said Daniel. "Also, my team has the same approach to meeting the needs of clients as I have. I'm proud to say we are all open and receptive to client concerns. When questions are raised outside of our comfort level, we refer the client to a specialist, just as is done when estate, accounting, or legal issues occur. The retirement specialist works with our clients directly, bringing an important added value into our relationship."

"The added value Daniel and his team offer is huge," Thelma said. "I've been asked several times to move my accounts to a different financial firm and advisor, but I won't. Daniel understands what I'm going through. He shares with me insightful books and articles and genuinely cares about my life-after-work success. It's because of our relationship that I'm staying put. You can't get me out of here with dynamite!"

"I'm impressed," Sally said. "But to be honest, Daniel, I'm somewhat financially illiterate. Though I've created a self-study plan to become more investment savvy, I'll need some serious handholding, everything from estimating my annual personal expenses during my retirement years to figuring out where the money will come from, be it my pension at Benson, my RRSP, personal savings, Canada Pension Plan, part-time work, or other sources. I also know I should better understand types of investments and which ones would be best for me. Can you help?"

"I'd really like to try, Sally," answered Daniel. "As part of our first meeting, I'd explore your thoughts and feelings about money, your unique character strengths and weaknesses, and how they factor into your investment plans. To be successful money managers, we all need to know ourselves. If risk bothers you, then lower risk investments may allow you to sleep at night. It's better to have your money in less risky investments such as government bonds or high-quality stocks. But I'm getting ahead of myself.

"I suggest we set up an exploratory meeting sometime next week, if you're willing. At the end of our session, you decide if you want to continue — no obligation."

"I like the idea," said Sally.

"How is Tuesday morning around 11 a.m.?"

"Done."

As Thelma and Sally were leaving Daniel's office, Sally turned to Daniel and asked, "I noticed the initials CFP after your name. What do they mean?"

"CFP means Certified Financial Planner. It's a financial designation for Canadian investment advisors. There are other designations. For instance, I'm currently earning my EPC, or Elder Planning Counsellor, accreditation."

"Thanks, Daniel. See you Tuesday."

As Sally and Thelma stood on the sidewalk, Sally thanked Thelma for introducing her to Daniel.

Sally added, "I'm looking forward to my meeting on Tuesday. I get the feeling Daniel and I will work well together. Thank you for today! You are a wonderful friend."

Ron and Charlotte began making contributions to their RRSPs in their early forties. Until that time, they spent their money on mortgage payments, providing for themselves and their three children, student debts, and other living expenses.

When they began seriously contributing to their retirement fund, they were afraid there would not be enough money for them to travel once a year to an exotic location, attend concerts, pay for Ron's golfing and Charlotte's photography hobby, help out their grandchildren with school, and enjoy life generally. Ron and Charlotte believed the hype at the time that they would need over $1 million in savings to live comfortably.

After interviewing several financial advisors, Ron and Charlotte met Lawrence. He was a financial advisor with whom they felt comfortable, and he assisted them in constructing a reasonably sized RRSP portfolio. Over the years, Lawrence met with them to review their progress and assisted them with budgeting based on their envisioned retirement needs. When Ron retired at sixty-five, he and Charlotte had over $700,000 set aside, which was enough to live comfortably and realize their retirement goals.

When asked about their progress, Ron and Charlotte admitted that without Lawrence's professional advice and encouragement, they probably wouldn't have made the advances they did. If they had handled their finances them-

selves, they figured they would have likely given up and convinced themselves they were destined to work their entire lives. They agreed that even though they were relatively good money managers, they needed the outside advice and direction from Lawrence to help them realize their long-term retirement vision.

EXERCISE 6

Net Worth Statement

Step 1

A. Liquid assets	Current Value
Chequing accounts	_____
Savings accounts	_____
GICs and T-bills	_____
Cash value of insurance policies	_____
Money market mutual funds	_____
Other liquid assets	
(e.g., money owed to you, tax refunds)	_____
Subtotal	_____

B. Long-term assets	
Mutual funds (non-money market)	_____
Stocks	_____
Bonds	_____
RRSPs/RRIFs/RESPs	_____
Company pension plan	_____
Subtotal	_____

C. Property assets	
Principal residence	_____
Vacation property	_____
Other real estate	_____
Vehicles	_____

Jewelry/art/collectibles/insurance/
    cash value   _____

Other property assets   _____

Subtotal   _____

Step 2

Liabilities

Mortgage (principal residence)   _____

Other mortgages   _____

Personal line of credit   _____

Auto loans   _____

RRSP loans   _____

Investment loans   _____

Credit cards   _____

Other loans   _____

Subtotal   _____

Step 3

Total Assets   _____

Total Liabilities   _____

= Your Net Worth   _____

EXERCISE 7

Cash Flow Statement

Complete the following cash flow statement forms. Evaluate
the numbers and determine what changes are necessary to
help achieve your retirement vision.

Cash Inflows	Monthly	Annually
Net salary (gross salary — taxes)	_____	_____
Interest income	_____	_____
Dividends	_____	_____
Capital gains	_____	_____
Rental income	_____	_____
Other income	_____	_____
RRSP/RRIF or pension income	_____	_____
Gov't benefits, tax refunds	_____	_____
Total cash inflows	_____	_____

Cash Outflows	Monthly	Annually
A. Living expenses		
Mortgage/rent	_____	_____
Property taxes	_____	_____
Heat	_____	_____
Water	_____	_____
Electricity	_____	_____
Cable TV/Internet	_____	_____
Telephone	_____	_____

	Monthly	Annually
Auto maintenance	_____	_____
Gas	_____	_____
Parking/transit	_____	_____
Groceries	_____	_____
Clothing	_____	_____
Childcare	_____	_____
Health and dental care	_____	_____

B. Debt payments

	Monthly	Annually
Loan payments	_____	_____
Personal line of credit	_____	_____
Credit cards	_____	_____
Other debt payments	_____	_____

C. Insurance plans

	Monthly	Annually
Home	_____	_____
Auto	_____	_____
Medical/dental	_____	_____
Life	_____	_____
Disability	_____	_____
Other insurance plans	_____	_____

D. Investment programs

	Monthly	Annually
Retirement contributions	_____	_____
Education savings plan	_____	_____
Emergency fund	_____	_____
Other investment programs	_____	_____

	Monthly	Annually

E. Discretionary expenses

	Monthly	Annually
Entertainment	_____	_____
Vacation	_____	_____
Subscriptions	_____	_____
Membership fees	_____	_____
Gifts	_____	_____
Charitable donations	_____	_____
Household purchases	_____	_____
Tuition	_____	_____

Total cash outflows _____ _____

Total cash outflows

	Monthly	Annually
Total living expenses	_____	_____
Total debt payments	_____	_____
Total insurance plans	_____	_____
Total investment programs	_____	_____
Total discretionary expenses	_____	_____
Total cash outflows	_____	_____

Total cash inflows minus _____ _____
Total cash outflows _____ _____

Total savings available for goals _____ _____

Notes:

_____

_____

_____

_____

Chapter 5

Health and Well-Being

One of the greatest discoveries a man makes, one of his great surprises, is to find he can do what he was afraid he couldn't do.
— Henry Ford

Summary:

Many people contemplating retirement believe it is a time to throw your cares away, just relax, and smell the roses. True, retirement is a time when you focus more on yourself, and it's a time when work priorities change. However, keeping healthy should be part of every person's journey into retirement.

Sally consults with her physician on her physical and mental health, including obtaining a full physical examination. She receives advice on making daily exercise a high priority as part of building and maintaining her overall health.

In this chapter, there is a list of possible symptoms of stress overload and techniques for coping.

And also there are three true stories and three exercises about your health (physical/diet/stress reduction).

Being healthy means having good physical, mental, and spiritual well-being. The interesting thing is when you are well, you have a feeling of vitality and personal confidence. And when you are unwell, you feel tired, lethargic, and down in spirit. Building a strong sense of wellness means spending time assessing your current state of health and asking: *What can I do to improve my well-being?* Obviously, you need to get regular physical check-ups and work with your doctor to develop a wellness plan that makes sense for your age and body. You need to create and follow a regular physical exercise routine. You also need to eat the right foods in the right proportions and develop a healthy frame of mind.

As part of Sally's retirement planning, she made an appointment with her doctor for a general physical check-up and to discuss how best to exercise.

"Sally, I'm ready to see you now," said Dr. Albert Lee-Jong. "I haven't seen you for a couple of months. How have you been doing?"

"I've been well and busy contemplating my life and what may lie ahead," replied Sally.

She then took several minutes to inform Dr. Lee-Jong of her upcoming termination from Benson & Sons and the prospect of looking for a new job, becoming retired, or possibly some combination. Sally also quickly outlined the work she has engaged in regarding creating a retirement vision and a balanced leisure lifestyle with the help of Thelma and others.

"Now I'm turning my attention to my wellness, including physical health," said Sally.

Dr. Lee-Jong expressed surprise about her release from Benson & Sons and then said, "Congratulations to you, Sally, for your proactive approach to the challenges that lie ahead. I wish more of my older patients were as constructive to life as you are. Far too many fail to plan and then wonder why their health deteriorates quickly."

"Doctor, as part of my planning, I need to reassess my exercise program, to choose activities that will increase my overall wellness."

"Okay, let's start with your blood pressure," replied Dr. Lee-Jong. "One hundred twenty-five over ninety, a little on the high side. Given all what you told me, I can understand the elevation, but I don't think it's anything to be worried about."

As Dr. Lee-Jong continued with his physical check-up, he asked, "Are there any physical activities you're afraid of? Are you a health club type of person? Do you like or dislike competitive sports? Are you more comfortable exercising on your own?"

Sally responded, "Until now, I've not had the time to devote to exercise. I know exercise improves cardiovascular health, lowers blood pressure, strengthens bones, builds muscle strength, and improves metabolism, but my job at Benson didn't leave me time, and whenever I thought of exercising, I was just too tired."

"From my experience, the key to developing the right program is to choose the right activities. If you don't enjoy what you're doing, your commitment to exercise will dwindle quickly. Luckily, there are hundreds of options that will elevate your heart rate, help with weight control, and build muscle mass. For some people, brisk walking is a good choice, while others prefer swimming. If you like to be outdoors in all types of weather, power walking or running are good exercises. However, if you dislike being out in the cold, an indoor calisthenics program would be better. What activities are you thinking of?"

"Doctor, I'm thinking of signing up for yoga and Pilates classes. Having a scheduled program seems more appropriate; it will force me to attend, plus I'll get to meet new people. I'm sure my classmates will provide me with encouragement, and the instructors will help with my goal setting."

"I think you're right. Once you get into a pattern of exercising and begin feeling the results, stay in tune. Give this part of your day top priority. When travelling, develop substitute exercises, and when illness strikes, tell yourself you will immediately return to your exercise regime when you are well enough to do so. Also, please share your training targets and desired weight goals with me to ensure they are realistic. One word of caution: I suggest you try a variety of different activities before committing to one or two. You may wish to sign up for a couple of yoga and Pilates classes, try brisk walking — whatever meets your fancy. Once you are totally convinced on your selection, then go ahead with your choice."

Heidi joined a tennis club on the advice of a friend as a way to be active and spend more time together. Upon signing up, she also purchased twelve lessons from the club pro. She bought herself an expensive tennis racket, several tennis outfits, top-of-the-line tennis shoes, and a few other accessories. She attended her first couple of tennis lessons and tried to enjoy the experience of learning a new game, but by the fourth lesson, she knew tennis wasn't for her. Heidi's tennis equipment now sits gathering dust in her closet, and her remaining paid lessons go unused.

When Bill was sixty-three, he contemplated retiring on his sixty-fourth birthday. He consulted with his financial planner and accountant, and each told him he had sufficient savings in his RRSP and other money accounts to be able to live a comfortable, though not lavish, retirement lifestyle.

Bill then turned his thoughts to his physical health. Though he considered himself to be in reasonable shape, he noticed he was getting tired faster and was taking more time than usual to recuperate from business trips and illnesses.

He then looked in the mirror and admitted to himself that he was not in the best physical condition. Right there, he made a commitment. If he was going to enjoy his retirement to its fullest, he would have to devote time and energy to becoming physically well.

After consulting with his physician, Bill began walking regularly. He set a goal of walking briskly for twenty minutes twice a week. At first, he thought he had set his goal too high, but he persisted despite his doubts. Within two weeks, he was walking thirty minutes three times a week. After four weeks, Bill was walking four times a week for forty minutes each time.

Bill was beginning to feel more energetic. He felt calmer and his overall confidence was increasing. He then bought five- and ten-pound dumbbells and began an easy weight-training program aimed at giving him better muscle tone.

After three months of walking and weight training, Bill was getting compliments on his appearance and energy level. People who had not seem him for some time observed that he looked and sounded healthier and younger than the old Bill.

Bill has now begun his retirement, and he says he has not felt better in his life. He keeps up his physical fitness and is training for a ten-kilometre run.

"Let's check your weight, Sally," said Dr. Lee-Jong. "We're just about finished with your physical."

As she stepped onto the weight scale, Sally said, "I'd like to drop about ten pounds. What can I do to make it happen?"

"For most people, as we get older, our nutritional needs change. Our metabolic rate, the speed at which our body burns calories, tends to decline. This means our body needs fewer calories to perform basic bodily functions such as walking, breathing, and talking. This also means needing to eat less or you may put on weight. I advise patients to develop a healthy diet; reduce their sugar, butter, and salt intake; and drink plenty of water. Also important, practice portion control at every meal. Here's a brochure outlining Canada's Food Guide. I'd encourage you to visit Canada's Food Guide website for food serving recommendations and meal planning tips. The website is listed on the brochure."

Dr. Lee-Jong handed Sally the brochure, which listed the website as food-guide.canada.ca.

"Just before you go, Sally, here's a requisition for blood tests I'd like you to have," said Dr. Lee-Jong. "The results will complete today's physical examination. My preliminary conclusion: For a person your age, you're in good shape. Let's get together again in, say, two weeks, at which time we'll review your blood test results. By the way, what are you planning to do to maintain your mental health?"

In our society, work is a defining feature of our daily lives and, to a large extent, our identity. It is more than the mental and physical tasks we perform. Work refers to the idea of being paid and engaged in activities that are productive. Ending your work life might not be an easy task because it makes up such a substantial part of your being. When you are working, your day is outer-directed. You focus on the task at hand and are normally busy at least eight hours a day. Time is measured by what you have accomplished, whether it's the report you completed, the clients you visited, the number of parts you produced, or the meetings you attended. When you retire, your day becomes inner-directed. You alone must plan your day and week. Success depends on your ability to find happiness in satisfying personal interests and pursuits, human relationships, and creative/mental activities.

As you approach retirement, you may have fears about losing self-identity or self-esteem, financial worries, and concerns about your health. For many newly minted retirees, the first months can be difficult because of our strong identification with "work." Just sitting back and reading the newspaper can result in a sense of guilt or anxiety because it doesn't feel like you are doing anything valuable or productive.

Upon entering retirement, you may experience butterflies, sweaty palms, upset stomach, and free-floating anxiety. First of all, relax. These are normal reactions to the new roles you are adopting. However, when stress builds up, your body reacts. Some of the possible symptoms of distress or stress overload include:

- Tension headaches
- Numerous colds, cold sores, and other viral disorders
- Skin rashes
- Ulcers and digestive disorders
- Irritability
- Insomnia
- Heart palpitations and high blood pressure
- Depression and grief
- Accidental injury due to inattention or distraction

"Thanks for asking, Doctor," said Sally. "I've been doing some reading on relaxation as one of the most powerful weapons we have to fight increased levels of stress. Of the techniques, including physical exercise, deep breathing, progressive muscle relaxation, and visualization, I'm drawn to using deep breathing: taking a deep breath through your nose, holding it for ten seconds, and releasing it slowly through your mouth, then repeating the process for five minutes."

"Sounds good, Sally," said Dr. Lee-Jong. "For me, when I experience increased stress, I visualize a sunny beach in the Caribbean with warm temperatures and blue water lapping onto the shore. I begin with a deep breath. I inhale slowly, hold for a few seconds, and then exhale through my mouth. I visualize my special place. I see the colours, hear the sounds, feel the warmth. I feel my tension and stress slip way."

Dr. Lee-Jong continued, "The use of a relaxation technique can do wonders. But I also advise my patients, when facing a stressful challenge or change, to talk to a friend or family member. Sharing concerns and asking for their thoughts often helps us learn new ways to handle tough situations. One's support network can provide sympathy, understanding, objectivity, knowledge, and encouragement. Remember, you are not alone. We shouldn't be afraid to ask for assistance, just as you would be willing to assist someone needing help. For me, I can easily talk to colleagues and get their support and understanding regarding the stressors I face and vice versa."

"Thanks, Doctor. See you in two weeks."

Harold thought he was ready for retirement. He had a good financial plan. He felt prepared and would often say, "Retirement — bring it on!"

When Harold retired, life was great for the first two months; it was like an extended vacation. Then he began to miss the office and, in particular, the praise from his colleagues and manager.

Even though Harold has retired from his work, his need for recognition continued. He missed the accolades, started to feel blue, and began to take his frustrations out on his wife. He criticized her housekeeping and grocery shopping. Each day he had one or more suggestions on how she could do her household activities better.

During one of Harold's "instructional" talks, his wife shouted, "When I married you, I didn't sign up for this! If you keep this up, I wonder if I'll want to stay around!"

As a result of his wife's concerns, Harold made an appointment with a counsellor. After a couple of sessions, he and the counsellor worked out a plan whereby Harold found an activity that gave him his needed recognition and praise. He is now volunteering with two non-profit organ-

izations, assisting them in revising their organizational structures. Both organizations are thrilled to have him as part of their team. In turn, he is receiving words of appreciation.

Harold and his wife now enjoy each other's company and are looking to the future.

EXERCISE 8

List the physical activities you currently do or would like to try. Write down why they appeal to you. For activities you would like to try, set a time frame for when you are going to start each activity. For activities you already engage in, set new goals for accomplishment.

Physical activities I do or would like to try:	Why I like or think I would like this activity:	My goal(s):
Brisk walking, 30 min. four times a week	*I'm not tied to a specific time or place*	*In two months I will walk five times a week, forty min. each time*
_____	_____	_____
_____	_____	_____
_____	_____	_____
_____	_____	_____
_____	_____	_____
_____	_____	_____
_____	_____	_____
_____	_____	_____

EXERCISE 9

Considering your current diet, what changes will you make to help you lead a more robust and enjoyable life? What foods are you going to eat more of? Which ones are you going to cut back on?

Changes I am going to make to my diet:

_____

_____

_____

_____

_____

_____

_____

_____

I am going to eat:

More of: Less of:
bran cereals   *donuts and muffins*
lean meats   *processed meats*
raw vegetables   *overcooked vegetables*

_____

_____

_____

_____

_____

_____

_____

_____

My target weight:

In one month: _____

In three months: _____

In six months: _____

EXERCISE 10

List your personal signs of stress (e.g., headaches, upset stomach, nervousness, inability to concentrate, etc.) and what you can do to reduce or eliminate your stress.

Signs of stress: **Actions to reduce or eliminate:**

_____

_____

_____

_____

_____

_____

_____

_____

Chapter 6

The Importance of Spirituality

Summary:

Spirituality is an important part of our health and well-being. Spirituality is about our existence, our relationships with ourselves, others, and the universe. It is something we experience that helps us understand life beyond what we can see, hear, and feel.

Studies conducted for groups such as the US National Interfaith Conference on Aging have related happiness, morale, and health to spirituality. People with less spirituality in general are not as happy or healthy as those with a high degree of spirituality.

Sally researches the importance of spirituality and creates her action plan to increase it.

This chapter includes a case study and exercise (addressing how to increase spirituality).

As we age, we become increasingly reflective and less concerned with material things. We are more interested in the satisfaction of life — through our creative work, religious beliefs, associations with our children and grandchildren, and connections with nature. Within the experience of aging, there is often an expanding sense of time in relation to quality of life.

As Sally was driving home from her appointment with her

physician, Dr. Albert Lee-Jong, she reflected on the results of her physical examination. She smiled when she remembered the words *you're in good physical shape*. She was also pleased with how succinctly she was able to describe her retirement vision and the planning steps to make it happen. She felt that the life-after-work puzzle pieces were falling into place. A comforting feeling! Sally was well underway to mapping her retirement life.

As she turned into her driveway, Sally took a moment to view her house and think about her children and how fortunate she was. "I am blessed," she thought. She then said a prayer of thanks, an unusual but seemingly comforting action for her.

After she entered her house, she googled: "retirement and spirituality." What she found were countless references.

"What can I do, I wonder, to increase my spirituality as part of my retirement planning?" thought Sally. As she quickly scrolled through the articles, she saw a repetition of similar statements. They were:

- Our spiritual side helps us appreciate and enjoy the life we lead.
- Spirituality can provide comfort when we face difficult life events — events older adults are more likely to encounter.
- Spirituality often provides us with tools to deal with what life throws our way.
- Spirituality can also strengthen faith in ourselves and our abilities, helping us create the life we want in retirement.

Regarding possible actions to increase one's spiritual qualities, Sally noted the following:

- Attending services in a house of worship
- Recognizing the power of prayer
- Extending and giving help to others in need
- Participating in activities such as drum circles
- Seeking and accepting help in dealing with life's challenges
- Taking time to reflect, meditate, or write in a journal
- Being in nature by walking in the woods, going fishing, etc.
- Appreciating the joy and beauty of the simple things in life

Sally sat on her sofa and thought for a moment. "If spirituality is an important part of a successful retirement, then it makes sense for me to nurture this part of me."

At that point, she resolved that she was going to consider finding suitable ways to do it and take action. She resolved to attend religious services at least once a month and "count her blessings" at least three times a week.

As Sally lived near a park with a nature trail, she mentally noted to include in her retirement a weekly walk through the woods. She thought, "Maybe Thelma would enjoy accompanying me."

As part of your retirement plan, think about how you can increase your spirituality and religious beliefs. Remember, there will be times in your life when having a strong spiritual connection will be comforting, especially when faced with a loss of mobility, a job loss, the illness or death of a loved one, or a personal or family disaster such as bankruptcy or divorce.

Marian and her husband, Blake, were enjoying their retirement. Both led active lives and were looking forward to many more years together.

Unfortunately, Blake was killed in an automobile accident. The shock was enormous. For several weeks, Marian was in an emotional tailspin. Throughout this period, her religious leader met with her, and together they prayed and spoke about Blake's life.

Though not a very religious woman, Marian found her faith provided her with an inner peace at a troubling time. She appreciated the time and insight provided by her religious leader, and today she has a renewed connection with her religion.

EXERCISE 11

Record your thoughts on how you can increase your spirituality and religious appreciation (e.g., regularly read scripture, attend religious services, take nature walks, think positively, etc.)

_____

_____

_____

_____

_____

_____

_____

Chapter 7

A Positive Attitude Leads to a Longer Retirement

Man alone, of all creatures of earth, can change his thought pattern and become the architect of his destiny.
— Spencer W. Kimball

Summary:

Fear, panic, and discomfort are common emotions experienced by people preparing for retirement. These emotions often occur because the pre-retiree is entering a new world, one with different circumstances, behaviours, and activities. A successful retirement takes courage, commitment, and desire. This involves changing routines, making new friends, trying new activities, and taking on new responsibilities.

Sally confides in Thelma about her sense of being overwhelmed by the changes she's facing. Thelma reassures Sally and mentors her in the importance of positive people, humour, and ability to laugh when things happen.

This chapter includes case studies. It also includes an attitude assessment as an exercise.

"Hi, Thelma, it's Sally calling. Do you have a minute to talk?"

"Hi, Sally, nice to hear your voice. I was just getting ready to leave for my weekly book club meeting. I've a few minutes to spare. What's up?"

"This morning, I was thinking about my retirement vision. For the most part, I'm happy with my balanced leisure lifestyle and the activities I plan to continue and those I will explore. I'm also giving thought to my health and well-being strategy, including my spirituality. I've got ideas on how to increase my social circle and the relationships with my family and friends. However, last night I felt overwhelmed about everything on my plate and had feelings these changes I'm contemplating may be too hard and I'll fail. My feeling of negativism worries me."

"Sally, your concerns are understandable and quite normal. I too wondered how successful I was going to be in life after work. However, I was determined to make the best of it. As part of my preparation for my newfound freedom, I researched the keys of living longer and thriving. I found that our attitude plays an enormous part in how successful we will be. Research has shown that seniors who continue to take an active part in their lives and view life in a positive light — those who don't see retirement as an end but as a beginning — live longer and are happier. These people gain the wisdom to enjoy their later years to the fullest."

"But you strike me as a very positive person in your retirement. You're cheerful and energetic and possess a spirit of adventure. How did you create such a positive attitude?"

Thelma laughed. "It didn't come easy. All through my life, I've naturally been an explorer; it's probably in part why I became a librarian. As a librarian, I've met thousands of people, including retirees. Many retirees came across to me as being grumpy old men and women who displayed negative behaviours, repelled others, and looked at the future with dread. Others exuded friendliness and optimism and seemed to attract like-minded people and viewed the future as a new and wonderful opportunity. I knew my choice and yelled out loud, "The past is the past. It came and it went. So what can I do now to influence my present and future?"

"What do I need to do to increase my positive attitude?"

"Sally, you're already taking action. You're beginning to build your vision of retirement and your plan for how to spend your time. You're giving thought to your finances and what you want from a financial advisor, and, as you told me a few moments ago, you're thinking about your health and well-being strategy. With your planning, you're weighing options and what will work for you and when you'll take action and how. The more positive images, questions, implicit beliefs, and positive self-talk you engage in, the more positive your mindset."

"You're right, Thelma. I'm beginning to become excited about life after work."

"And if you catch yourself drifting into a negative mindset, stop and refocus on the positive — and give me a call so we can talk through your trip-up.

"Make sure you surround yourself with positive people; seek humour in situations, and laugh at yourself when things happen. Remember, Sally, you bring into retirement all your experience, knowledge, and intuition — all the skills that served you well up to now. Trust your abilities!"

"You know, I believe I can do this — I really don't want to be one of the grumpy old people no one likes to be around. Thanks, Thelma. Enjoy your book club meeting."

Roger looked only at his past and refused to welcome the challenges of retirement. When he turned sixty-five, he retired from his job and began receiving a pension. Soon after, he became bitter. He spoke only of his job and his work buddies, whom he saw less and less. His negative attitude about "growing old" and his complaints have driven away most of his friends. His children visit only when they have to, and Roger spends many hours alone. He has turned his back on what could have been the best time of his life.

Linsey accepts the challenges of retirement. When she left the workforce, her retirement vision was, and still is, to make good things happen. She welcomes each day and treats it as an adventure. As part of her journey, she seeks out new people to meet and get to know, plans one major trip a year, and spends time with her grandchildren. She attends community concerts and often drives in the countryside with her camera, looking for scenes to photograph.

Sheilagh recently became a resident of an assisted-living community housing complex. From day one, she ensured to sit and eat her meals with different people each time. During the meals, she asks questions of her tablemates to determine their interests and thoughts on public affairs, and she asks for advice and opinions on all matter of topics. She also enjoys playing piano and each week presents a short concert or sing-along for the residents. Through her actions, everyone knows Sheilagh and appreciates her positive and warm personality.

EXERCISE 12

Complete the following attitude assessment. Read each pair of statements and rate yourself from 10 to 1. Circle the number representing where you currently are on the spectrum. Upon completion, review your selected numbers. Note the areas with low scores (4, 3, 2, or 1). What changes do you want to make to increase your attitude in each of these areas?

Attitude Assessment	High	Low
Retirement is going to be the most exciting part of my life	10 9 8 7 6 5 4 3 2 1	I dread my retirement
There are many exciting opportunities	10 9 8 7 6 5 4 3 2 1	Everything is downhill after retirement
I want to stay in control and be active	10 9 8 7 6 5 4 3 2 1	I just want to withdraw from it
I will turn challenges into opportunities	10 9 8 7 6 5 4 3 2 1	I am not up to coping with change
I intend to expand my sense of humour	10 9 8 7 6 5 4 3 2 1	There's nothing fun about getting old

Retirees have advantages over others	10 9 8 7 6 5 4 3 2 1	Retirees have no advantages in society
I can make new friends	10 9 8 7 6 5 4 3 2 1	I'm obsolete, and no one wants to know me
Retirement is the best time of my life	10 9 8 7 6 5 4 3 2 1	This is the time to give up
Now I can use my creative talents	10 9 8 7 6 5 4 3 2 1	I have nothing to give and contribute

Based on your responses, write out your action plan to increase your positive attitude towards retirement. Consider the following statements and feel free to include them in your plan:

- I will try to meet one new person each week.
- I will laugh more and find the humour in situations.
- I will view my retirement glass as half full, not half empty.

_____

_____

_____

_____

_____

_____

_____

Chapter 8

Choosing Where to Live

Summary:

Considering where you will spend your time is every bit as important as considering how you will spend your time. Many retirees hope their current home will meet their retirement needs, or, rather, it's more accurate to say many retirees prefer to stay in their current home.

Sally discusses possibly selling her home or downsizing with Michelle Spears, an experienced realtor. Michelle explains to her how a reverse mortgage works.

This chapter's exercise will get you to list the advantages and disadvantages of moving.

Sally loved her backyard and, particularly, her flower garden. She enjoyed sitting on her deck on a warm spring or summer evening, gazing at the wide variety of plants she painstakingly tended and nurtured.

One late afternoon, when Sally was transplanting a lilac bush from its position under a pine tree to a more open location, she heard her neighbour Wilson call over the fence.

"Hi, Sally. How are you?"

"Fine, Wilson. Just moving this lilac so it gets more sun."

"How's your retirement planning going?"

Two weeks ago, Sally had told Wilson about her pending layoff from Benson and the discussions with Thelma and others aimed at preparing her for possible retirement.

"With all my soul-searching and my work to craft my retirement plan, I'm thinking about my living accommodations," Sally said. "Recently, my financial advisor recommended selling my home and moving to a lower priced area. He said I could use the capital gains to enhance my retirement spending."

"How do you feel about your home?" Wilson asked.

"I feel safe and secure here. And it represents the life Pierre and I had for many years. I own the house free and clear and so don't have mortgage payments. And I love my garden."

"Leaving a home you're comfortable in is an emotional decision. When Mable, God bless her soul, passed away, I immediately thought about selling my house and moving to a condo. Sure glad I didn't. A friend of mine advised me to reconsider moving and not to rush into any decisions. Greatest advice she could have given me. You might be interested in speaking with a friend of mine, Michelle Spears. She operates a small real estate firm. I'm sure she would be pleased to talk about your options — staying where you are, using a reverse mortgage, or downsizing."

"Yes, I'd like to meet her but with the understanding I'm not obligated to take action until I'm ready."

Wilson pulled out his phone and called Michelle. After some friendly banter, he mentioned Sally and her desire to explore the question of where to live. He then gave Sally the phone, and together Michelle and Sally arranged to meet in Michelle's office the next morning.

It was a beautiful morning when Sally arrived at Michelle's office.

"Welcome," said Michelle. "It's such a glorious day today, though I heard on the radio as I was driving in that the weather forecasters are predicting rain for tomorrow. Would you like a coffee?"

"Yes, please. One sugar," Sally said. "How long have you been in the real estate business?"

"I'll be celebrating my tenth anniversary in August. I used to be a paralegal in a large law firm, but the office politics wore me out. My move from law to real estate was the best decision of my life. I get to meet pleasant people like you, and I get a kick out of solving people's housing needs."

"The other day, I saw an ad on TV selling reverse mortgages. I'm not sure I totally understand what a reverse mortgage is. Would you explain it to me?"

"Sure," said Michelle. "With a reverse mortgage, a homeowner takes out a loan based on the equity and market value of the home. Any current mortgage is paid off with the proceeds, and the bank makes either a lump-sum or monthly payments to the homeowner with the remaining funds. Alternatively, the homeowner can set up a line of credit with the proceeds of the reverse mortgage to draw on when necessary. The homeowner retains the title to their home and remains responsible for paying property taxes and home insurance. The homeowner is required to have mortgage insurance for the reverse mortgage loan."

"To qualify for a reverse mortgage, the homeowner must continue to live in the residence as their main home. The interest rate on the loan is variable, and the reverse mortgage doesn't have to be repaid as long as the home-owner stays in the home.

"For some people, having a reverse mortgage works well, but for others, not so well. One advantage of a reverse mortgage is the money can be used for any purpose, such as home repair and maintenance, long-term care, medical needs, or paying debt. On the flip side, in most cases, the home must be sold to pay back the reverse mortgage, and there may not be any money left for the heirs."

"At this point, taking out a reverse mortgage doesn't sound like a good option for me," Sally said.

"Tell me about your home. Are you satisfied with the size? What is the layout of the place and what are the maintenance costs? What's your neighbourhood like? Are there restaurants, cafés, community centres, fitness centres, grocery stores, medical and dental care, and public transportation nearby?"

Sally described her home and neighbourhood's amenities.

"Think five years into the future. Does your home still appeal to you?" Michelle asked.

"In five years, my two sons, Jerry and Michael, will be married and maybe fathers, and Emily, my daughter, will be graduating from university. I hope I will have met someone special who is maybe living with me. We would be travelling and enjoying each other's company. When I look at my home five years from now, the question is: *Do I like where I live or am I simply used to it?*"

"How do you feel about moving within the next five years?"

"It's something I should research. Do I make renovations so I can remain in my home? Do I move to a smaller house in my neighbourhood, move into a condo or apartment when the kids are gone, or buy a cottage on a lake? The beauty of it is I'm not in a rush and can take my time."

"Regardless where you're living, you'll probably want to do some decluttering, especially if you decide to move to a smaller space. Many of my clients, when they've bought a smaller property, take all their possessions with them into the new home. My advice is to examine your furniture and other goods with a critical eye. Make decisions about the big pieces first. Go through your clothes, books, housewares, etc. The next couple of years is the time to unload other people's things, including items you've stored for your children. Have a garage sale and make donations to charities. One client recently hired a professional organizer; this reduced her stress and helped her reach her goals more quickly."

"I think I can sort my belongings myself. I'm fairly good at organizing and have a disciplined way of thinking once I get started with a project. There are some things I have that I'm not sure I'd part with. I could put those into storage. That might help me determine if I really want or need them."

"As part of your research, would you like me to appraise your home? No obligation. That way you'll have a ballpark figure in mind if and when you contemplate any change. Also, I'll supply you with information on reverse mortgages, brochures on condos being built in your neighbourhood, and, for fun, the hot spots around the world where some retirees are taking up residence."

"Thanks, Michelle. I don't want you to put yourself out,

as I'm not in a rush to move."

"No, not at all. Consider it our research project. And when you decide, I'd appreciate an opportunity to work with you."

Sally promised to call Michelle later in the month after she had a chance to look at the documents.

EXERCISE 13

List the advantages and disadvantages of moving:

1. Staying where I am.

Advantages	Disadvantages
I love my home.	*Homeownership is expensive.*

_____

_____

_____

_____

_____

_____

_____

2. Renting.

Advantages	Disadvantages
No maintenance problems.	*Rent increases.*

_____

_____

_____

_____

_____

_____

3. Moving to a condo.

Advantages   Disadvantages
Usually safer than a private   *Bureaucratic rules to*
home.   *follow, association politics.*

_____
_____
_____
_____
_____
_____
_____

4. Buying a mobile home.

Advantages   Disadvantages
Less capital investment.   *Neighbours too close.*

_____
_____
_____
_____
_____
_____

5. Retirement centre.

Advantages   Disadvantages
Offers greater protection.   *Fewer young people*
                                    around.

_____
_____
_____

_____
_____
_____
_____
_____

6. Move to the cottage.

Advantages   Disadvantages
Close to nature.   *Away from needed
                                medical services.*

_____
_____
_____
_____
_____
_____

7. Settle in a warm climate.

Advantages   Disadvantages
Don't have to shovel snow.   *Not regularly seeing
                                grandchildren.*

_____
_____
_____
_____
_____
_____

Chapter 9

The Best Time to Retire

All of us were meant to be happy and successful. Life is more than a two-week vacation once a year. It is, and can be, exactly what you want it to be. There are no limits except those you put on yourself.
— Thomas D. Willhite

Summary:

As part of any retirement plan, there is a need to seriously consider the best time of year to retire. There are financial implications, but one should also consider the season at the time of entering life after work. But be cautious. Be sure to check the programs at your company before considering your resignation.

In this chapter, Thelma advises Sally to fully understand her company benefits prior to leaving Benson & Sons. And Sally reveals her plan to getting retirement off on the right foot.

There is an exercise in this chapter about choosing the best time of year to retire.

"Hi, Thelma. I hope you don't mind me calling with another question concerning my retirement planning."

"Hi, Sally. No of course not. The planning process is something you don't do in five minutes. For me, it took over a month to think about all the various aspects. Then, when I thought I had a realistic vision of retirement, I explained my vision to four very close friends, who then asked me questions, such as 'What was your thinking about this?' and 'Tell me more about your decision making on that.' Their questions helped me revisit my vision and either clarify it more or accept my description. As a result, I had a well-structured vision of my retirement I was comfortable with and excited to put into action. So, what's on your mind?"

"This morning, I woke up wondering whether there is a best time of year to retire," said Sally. "Are there financial implications to think about? What about the seasons of the year?"

"Yes, Sally, the timing of your retirement can prove to be important. One aspect to consider is your employer benefit programs. I believe you told me Benson is continuing your benefits for six months after your last day. One question you should clarify with them is whether any cost-of-living increase on your pension in that six months will be added on. And review your benefits with the human resources department so you have a clear understanding on the details of each. For instance, if you require major dental care in the six-month period, is it covered?

"Sally, do you have any vacation time owing to you?"

"Yes, three weeks, which I didn't take last year."

"Make sure that time is added into your severance package, or ask the HR people if you can use up your vacation days prior to the start of your severance date. For employees preparing to retire, the first week of January may be appealing to begin their retirement, especially if they are carrying more than the maximum accrual for vacation.

They could get paid for the total as long as they retire before the end of the first pay period in January. Retiring in January also gives you the entire tax year to absorb any lump-sum payoff.

"Tax considerations and the best time to retire are different for each individual. It's worthwhile to meet with your accountant regarding taxes and get her advice.

"Since you will be leaving Benson at the end of the month, it's important to have your retirement plan completed together with activities and events to coincide with the season. Those who retire in January may start with a trip to the sunny south or take a ski holiday. Retiring in the spring and the prospect of gardening and being outdoors may be appealing. If someone owns a cottage, the summer months may be the time of choice for retiring. The fall months may also be ideal, as this is a time of completion, celebration, and planning for the New Year. What are you planning to do to get your retirement off on the right foot?"

"Right now, when I leave Benson, I'm envisioning taking an Alaskan cruise," Sally declared. "It's something I've always dreamed about and has been on my bucket list forever. It's time to strike it off the list and add the experience to my life. Being at sea will permit me time to consider how important work will be as part of my retirement."

"Sounds like a plan."

EXERCISE 14

While considering possible cost-of-living payments, vacation payoff, tax considerations, and the seasons, choose the best time of year to begin your retirement and list the reasons for your choice.

_____

_____

_____

_____

_____

_____

_____

_____

Chapter 10

Relationships in Retirement

A friend is someone who sees through you and still enjoys the view.
—Wilma Askinas

Summary:

Most people recognize that when they retire, the relationships they have with people from work will change drastically or become a distant memory. To be successful socially, you need to work at keeping up with current friends and be proactive in seeking new ones.

At retirement, the relationship that often changes is the one you have with your spouse or partner. For those who are single, there is a more serious need to have a supportive social circle. Parenting and other caregiving in retirement is another challenge.

In this chapter, Thelma and Sally explore the need for a strong social circle, being retired and single, and caring for Sally's mother.

And there are nine case studies and four exercises in this chapter.

As Sally sat at her desk at work, she looked around the office and noted her workmates busy at their daily responsibilities. To her right was Margaret, a colleague for more than two years. Sally thought, "When I leave the company, I'll miss my morning chats with Margaret and the adventures of her two cats. Then there is Charlotte, who always has something more important to talk about, in her mind, than I do. Oh, Bob, what a flirt: Mr. Casanova. And then there's Wang. What a sweet, considerate person. I'll miss them all."

Sally then thought, "As part of my planning, I must remain proactive in meeting new people and forming friendships. Among the people who are close to me now are Margaret, Thelma, Samantha and Arlene from the book club, my children, and Bruce, a friend from high school I recently reconnected with."

Sally continued thinking along these lines: "One way to enlarge my social circle is to let those in my social circle know how important they are to me. Also, I should tell them what is happening and that I want to expand my circle of friends even more. Maybe I should join some groups such as Probus, the social organization for people fifty-five and over."

When Alice and her husband, Ron, retired, they moved from Toronto to Charlottetown. They had visited Prince Edward Island on vacation and loved the province. Once settled in their new home, they made an extensive effort to introduce themselves to their neighbours. They joined a local church and each Sunday attended the coffee gathering held after the service. They became members of the local bridge club and several other organizations. In a short while, Alice and Ron had a new social circle of friends and felt very much at home.

Cy is constantly rewarding those in his social circle. He recognizes the birthdays of his financial advisor, accountant, and life insurance agent. When asked why he takes the time to remember their birthdays, Cy's answers, "These people are important to me. They play a critical role in my life and help me keep my financial and personal affairs in order."

Exercise 15

List the people you consider part of your social circle. Outline what rewards you will give to signify their importance to you.

My Social Circle
My dad

Suitable Rewards
Call at least once a week

_____	_____
_____	_____
_____	_____
_____	_____
_____	_____
_____	_____
_____	_____

Spousal/Partner Relationships

At retirement, the relationship that often changes is the one you have with your spouse or partner. In the early and middle years of marriage, couples normally don't spend a lot of time together. They are busy making a living, raising a family, and fixing up a home. In a recent survey, it was found the average married couple spends only three or four hours a week together without the children. And they often spend that time simply watching TV together.

Due to today's hectic pace, we tend to develop our own separate schedules and routines around work, family, and home demands. Then retirement comes, and it's a time to relax and enjoy the fruits of our labour, which includes spending quality time with our partner. It's supposed to be the time when we enrich our relationship, when we do things and go places together.

However, a relationship filled with good times is not something that just happens. Like all other aspects of retirement, it requires planning and effort. As part of your plan, it's important to recognize that you and your partner have built up your own space and privacy needs. Each of you needs time to pursue your own interests, hobbies, and tasks or to just "chill out alone." One train of thought is if you were apart from your partner eight hours a day during your working days, you should plan to be apart approximately four hours a day in retirement. This gives each partner their own time and space. Be sure to talk with each other about your needs and agree on how those needs can be fulfilled.

Frank and Amber agreed that when Frank retired, he would participate in activities outside the home three mornings every week. They also agreed that while Amber had the house to herself, she would indulge in her hobby, pottery. The couple agreed that they would walk to their favourite pastry shop for coffee twice a week and have a date night once a week. This arrangement has worked out well, and Frank and Amber recommend their time and space plan to other retired couples.

As part of your planning, it's important for you and your spouse to talk about what retirement means in terms of roles and responsibilities. Create mini job descriptions and outline the dates, duties, responsibilities and authorities of each partner.

Before Dick and Anastasia began their retired life, they discussed who would be responsible for what in retirement. It was mutually decided that Dick would do the grocery shopping, snow shovelling, and raking. He would make the bed each morning, prepare for dinner, and do several other domestic chores. For her part, Anastasia would do the cleaning and vacuuming as well as the washing, drying, folding, and ironing of their clothes. They agreed that household decorating would be done together. This sharing of responsibilities helped Dick and Anastasia build a harmonious working relationship without one partner feeling they were doing the lion's share of the work.

For some couples, however, there is no prior discussion about what retirement means to them and who will take care of the numerous life tasks. This often leads to disastrous results.

Peter was a senior manager for a utility company and was used to telling others what he wanted them to do. His wife, Pam, was a successful advertising executive. When they retired, both looked forward to a life of relaxation, fun, and spending time together in their garden. However, three months into retirement, Peter began to criticize Pam's gardening techniques. He commented on her spacing of the plants, the way she waters and fertilizes, her pruning, and other gardening flaws. His nitpicking continued until Pam got so angry one day that she stormed out the door. Peter was shocked when a friend told him that she might not come back.

After several discussions with a counsellor, Peter and Pam have reconciled. Peter recognized his need for con-

trol and worked at reducing it. He got a part-time job as a dog trainer and has learned not to criticize Pam's gardening skills.

The essential elements of a happy relationship are feeling valued, being appreciated, and being loved. When a couple lacks any one of these, the relationship suffers and the partners drift apart. Accepting the status quo slowly wears away at a couple's intimacy and bond.

Though it is easy to take each other for granted, the preparation for retirement provides you and your spouse with an opportunity to assess and enhance your relationship. Are you thoughtful? Do you express appreciation? Do you have a sense of fun and adventure? These traits, among others, add to the quality of your relationship and the satisfaction level between you and your partner.

Don't fall into the trap of believing everything must be okay if your partner isn't complaining. Keep the communication lines open and take time to listen to your spouse. Encourage discussion about each other's issues and concerns with the mindset of finding solutions.

If you tend to be indifferent about your appearance, thinking it's not a big deal, take the time and make an effort to look good — not only when you're going out but also when lounging around the house.

To add spice to your relationship, do little romantic things such as buy flowers or treat your partner to lunch. Say thank you to recognize what they do for you and your relationship. Spend quality time together and share fun activities. Relationships are like a garden: They require regular care and feeding if they are to grow and become fruitful.

Exercise 16

List some acts of kindness and appreciation you can do for your spouse to let them know how much you love them. (For example, make the coffee/tea in the morning, help with meal preparation, or wash their car.)

Little Acts of Kindness

_____

_____

_____

_____

_____

_____

_____

_____

Retired and Single

After a two-week absence, Sally and Thelma met again at Chuck's for coffee.

"Oh, it's so nice to see you again, Thelma. I've missed our time together, especially with everything that's going on."

"It's wonderful to see you again. Today, let's try the pumpkin spice latte."

"Great idea."

As they walked to the coffee counter, Thelma asked, "By the way, how was your visit with your doctor?"

"I'm in good shape for a person my age. I passed my physical, and my blood tests came back from the lab and everything is normal, including my cholestoral levels. Dr. Lee-Jong suggested I lose a few pounds and pay attention to my increased anxiety. Since my check-up, I've read articles on diet and weight control and started practicing meditation. With my meditation, at first I fell asleep within two or three minutes. Now I'm getting the hang of it, letting my body relax but not dropping off into a deep sleep. I'm looking into joining a Pilates class to keep myself in good physical shape.

"Also, as part of my mental health planning, I'm going to continue with my love of crossword puzzles and word games. I've recently downloaded several board games, including chess and checkers, onto my iPad."

"Good for you, Sally, for taking action so quickly."

"Another piece of my health plan that Dr. Lee-Jong suggested is addressing my spirituality," said Sally.

"Yes, there are many published reports demonstrating the benefits of a robust spiritual life when retired."

"My plan is to return to my church and take time out of each day to be thankful for all the gifts life has given me, including my health, family, and friends.

"I've rewritten my vision of retirement, keeping in mind your advice and what Rique, Silvani, and Gomad have said. As this stage, I'm seriously considering becoming semi-retired. I've met with Daniel, and he's reviewed my investments, and I now have a revised financial plan that will support my retirement vision.

"My neighbour Wilson introduced me to Michelle Spears, a realtor who is coming to appraise my house next week. And yesterday I was reviewing my social circle and making plans on meeting new people. Then, of course, there were my calls to you for continued advice."

"Wow," said Thelma. "You've been one very busy person. Congratulations. This is wonderful. And by the way, you look much more relaxed and at ease."

"You're right, Thelma. Without your help and mentoring, I'm not so sure I could have coped. I owe you such a debt of gratitude."

"Oh, and by the way, Mark Grier has a copy of Benson & Sons' severance package, and he is in discussion with Benson's human resources department, clarifying my company benefits during the six-month coverage time and negotiating for a higher settlement amount."

"That's wonderful news. So, what can I help you with today?"

"When I was redrawing from my social circle, I was plagued by the question of being single in retirement."

"This is a situation many of my girlfriends and work colleagues have talked about quite a bit. As single people, one question we have to ask ourselves, 'What do I need to do so I can be better situated to enjoy a happy and secure retirement?' When I think of all the conversations, there are several ways you can, in my opinion, thrive as a single person in retirement."

"What are they?"

"The first one is to cultivate, as you are doing, a support network. Friends we can call to invite for dinner, go out for coffee, or just chat on the phone. We also need to identify people who can be available to occasionally check in and help with tasks such as driving to appointments and assisting with shopping and chores when we are unable. You are healthy and independent now, and you may not require support from others for many years to come, but an emergency could happen at any time, so it's a good idea to have a network in place."

"My sons and daughter could help me if I need assistance," Sally said.

"What if in a few years' time Jerry and Michael have their own families and Emily is away on business? Who's going to help you?"

"Good point, Thelma. Of course, I'd be there for you."

"And I for you. Don't forget your neighbours as part of your network."

"I know, as part of my retirement plan, I've got to be actively seeking out people. I'll be contacting Probus in the next couple of weeks as a possible way to meet others my age. I'm also thinking of taking a couple of courses at the community college for both mental stimulation and meeting people who have similar interests."

"Good for you, Sally," said Thelma. "One word of advice. If you can't find a friend to go with you, don't let that stop you from going to a restaurant, movie, concert, or museum or on a day trip on your own. I know this is a big adjustment, especially if you are newly single after years of marriage, but the effort is worth it.

"Another point my friends and workmates have explored, is considering alternative living arrangements. If you are accustomed to living alone, you may be able to continue long into retirement. But the time will come when living with others or living in a close-knit community becomes desirable or even necessary. One option I've considered is moving to a co-housing community with private homes clustered around a shared space. Shared spaces typically feature a common house, which may include a large kitchen and dining area, laundry facilities, and recreational spaces. Neighbours commit to being part of a community for everyone's benefit. They collaboratively plan and manage community activities and share resources such as tools and lawnmowers.

"Then there is the option of simply sharing a home with two or more unrelated adults — like on *The Golden Girls*. There are several websites that can help you find roommates."

"One of my concerns is travelling by myself," said Sally.

"That is a major concern for a lot of us," said Thelma. "Travelling solo might be one of the biggest challenges you face as a single retiree, especially if you've been accustomed to travelling with your spouse, like you and Pierre did. But the fact that you're single is no reason to abandon your travel dreams. When you travel by yourself, you can set your own itinerary. You won't have to compromise with a travel companion who doesn't want to do the same things you do. If you feel tired one day, you can relax without being concerned that you're depriving your travel partner of anything.

"If you have some reservations about travelling alone, begin slowly. Start with day trips in your car or weekend trips to a nearby city. Cruise ships and group tours are options worth considering. When travelling solo, exercise common sense and follow safety precautions. If you're exploring on your own, leave a note with your day's itinerary in your hotel room so that if you don't return, the authorities will know where to start looking for you. Research maps, transportation schedules, and prices before you venture out so you appear confident. Learn how much a taxi should cost, and verify the amount with the driver before you begin the ride."

"Thanks for your information."

"Hey, the next time my single friends and I get together, would you like to join us? I'm sure you'll have fun, and they're full of ideas on how to live a super single life."

Exercise 17

As a single person:

1. What steps will I take to increase my support network?

_____

_____

_____

_____

_____

_____

_____

_____

2. What am I planning to do to find new friends?

_____

_____

_____

_____

_____

_____

_____

3. What activities will I engage in to be around others when I'm by myself (e.g., concerts, craft shows, movies, zoos, etc.)?

_____

_____

_____

_____

_____

_____

_____

_____

4. Actions to check out regarding travelling solo?

_____

_____

_____

_____

_____

_____

_____

5. How will I make my dining solo a sensual experience?

_____

_____

_____

_____

_____

_____

_____

6. How will I stay active (e.g., hiking, jogging, swimming, yoga, etc.)?

_____

_____

_____

_____

_____

_____

_____

_____

7. How will I take care of myself (treating myself on a regular basis) (e.g., gourmet tea or coffee, fresh flowers, a scented candle, soaps, special interest magazine, etc.)?

_____

_____

_____

_____

_____

_____

_____

_____

Caring for an Elderly Parent

"How's your mom doing?" asked Thelma.

"She is doing well right now, thanks," answered Sally. "She seems comfortable in the home. When I visit her, I ask if anything worries her and if she feels safe. I can tell from observing that the staff respect her and have gone out of their way to introduce Mom to other residents. Mom really likes Noel, the nurse on the afternoon shift.

"The other day I reviewed Mom's day-to-day routine with Margarette, the head nurse for those with Alzheimer's. Margarette has not seen any signs of depression and says Mom appears to be making the transition smoothly to living in the home."

"What about the overall environment?" asked Thelma. "I mean such things as cleanliness, lighting, odours, safety hazards, and the like?"

"When I visit, I make it a point to get a feel for the home. Are the staff caring enough? Are they affectionate, genuine, and helpful? Do I hear music and laughter? Does Mom appear settled and not just sitting in front of a TV? A couple of times I've dropped by at night, and each time I was greeted by the staff in a courteous manner and invited to join several staff members for cocoa. I'm happy for Mom."

"How are you coping?"

"Mom's happy, but I'm not."

"What's wrong, Sally?"

"I feel guilty that I was not able to care for her. I also feel guilty about asking others to help, and at the same time I feel guilty about not asking for help. I worry I made the wrong decision and that I've failed my mom. I probably don't sound logical."

"You are not alone. Many people, especially daughters, struggle with or regret a decision to place their loved one in a care facility. Realize that you didn't cause your mom to get ill. She would continue to suffer whether you were the sole caregiver or the nursing home staff. The professional care your mom is receiving is necessary for her safety and comfort and for you to have some life apart from caregiving.

"Your job is to provide the right care for your mom and at this stage of her illness. You made the right choice for everyone. Putting anyone into a new environment can be an uncomfortable and even distressing experience. Suddenly, while at their most vulnerable, we 'ask' our parents to form new acquaintances, trust new professional caregivers, navigate new schedules, and acclimate to new environments. At the same time, we, as their children, are thrust into primary decision-making roles and can only hope our parent will make the best of the new situation."

"You get it. Thanks, Thelma."

Thelma reached out and hugged Sally.

"I'm here for you whenever you want to talk," Thelma whispered. "I'd like to meet your mom the next time you go to see her."

"Absolutely."

Costs of Care

- Take a financial inventory. Have a family meeting and take stock of the financial resources available. Pensions, Social Security/CPP, and personal investments can help soften the financial burden for adult children.
- Consider tapping home equity to pay for caregiving ex-

penses. Sell the home or downsize elderly parents into a smaller space and use the funds for long-term care. Investigate implementing a reverse mortgage.

- Long-term care policies can help with eldercare costs.
- Nursing homes are not the only option. Parents might move in with their adult children or use a home health aide. The next level might be an assisted-living facility that offers an array of services for independent living, and even different levels of care within the same facility.

Jan's elderly father lives alone. At present he is able to do his housekeeping, shopping, and gardening, but he has recently fallen several times resulting in short stays at the hospital. His eyesight is also failing, and his arthritis is making him less agile. Jan and her husband, Nick, know it will not be long before some action will be needed.

Jan and Nick have explored the options of keeping her father in his current residence, moving him to a nursing home, or having him live with them. After discussing the situation, they both agreed to hire a housekeeper for him for the first year. They would then convert part of their home into a self-contained suite to provide privacy for him and an opportunity for them to assist when needed. Prior to making this decision, Jan and Nick consulted with Jan's father, who agreed it was the best alternative.

EXERCISE 18

Considering the age and health of your parents, what actions do you envision occurring in the next five years? Will your parents or spouse's parents be able to live on their own or will home care or nursing care be required? Would or could you and your spouse have a parent share your home?

_____

_____

_____

_____

_____

_____

_____

_____

Chapter 11

Being Remembered: Your Legacy

Summary:

Successful retirees give considerable thought to how they want to be remembered. They suggest imagining being ninety, ninety-five, or a hundred years old. In old age, when you look back on your life, what will stand out as your best accomplishments? When others think of you, what will their memories be?

This is not an exercise in conceit; rather, it can help you identify what's truly important in your life. This is part of what's needed to imagine, plan, implement, and maintain a successful retirement.

In this chapter, there are two case histories and two exercises.

Sally and Thelma finished their lattes as they sat in two overstuffed chairs on the upper level at Chuck's.

Sally said, "Last night, I was jotting down thoughts on how I'd like to be remembered when I'm ninety or ninety-five years old. This got me thinking of some actions I'd need to take to make my legacy a reality."

"Like what?" asked Thelma.

"Though Jerry and Michael are still relatively young and single, I want to be remembered as a fabulous grandma. If blessed with grandchildren, I will try my best to attend my grandchildren's sporting events. I will help out at their school. I will take them to the park, play with them in the backyard, and join them on campouts. I want to play an important role in their life."

"Sounds like a beautiful legacy. Any other things you have planned for your legacy?"

"There's one more, and that's appreciating my friends more than in the past. Thelma, I consider you to be a good friend, and whether you like it or not, I intend to regularly let you know it." Sally laughed.

"And there's another action I'm planning as part of my legacy," said Sally. "I'm intending to leave a gift of family history to Jerry, Michael, and Emily. I plan to record my knowledge about myself, my mom and dad, brother, sisters, aunts, uncles, cousins, and other family members. I will be recording my knowledge of each, including where they were born, when, notes on who they are or were, occupations, hobbies, and interests. Also, very crucial is information about our family's medical history, facts that could be lifesaving for my children, grandchildren, and other family members."

"Sounds wonderful. I'm sure your children will appreciate your gifts to them."

Many years after I am gone, I'd like my love for animals to live on. My financial planner knows this and has helped me identify certain assets to give to my favourite shelter after I have passed. It won't matter that those assets are not nearly enough to put my name on a building. And in the meantime, I give my time at the shelter three days a week, teaching new volunteers.

— Elsa T., former newspaper journalist

Elsa's love for animals has current benefits for her as well:

1. She worked with her financial advisor on what amounts to an estate plan.
2. She has a social circle of friends who work and volunteer at the animal shelter.
3. Volunteering adds structure and a sense of fulfillment to her life.
4. Teaching volunteers continually broadens her social circle and helps keep her brain challenged and healthy.

Recently, I met a retiree named George. As it was Christmas time, we talked about the holidays, including gifts that meant a great deal to us. George told me of a gift he was creating for his son. He hopes his son will remember and treasure the gift for years to come.

George had purchased a small voice recorder, which he carries with him, and as he recalls things about his past or facts involving his family, he records his thoughts. Over the past two months, he has recorded family information, including names, birthdates, deaths, marriages, and remembrances and stories he heard from his parents and family members. To date, George has filled four tapes and is amazed with what he remembers at the oddest times.

For example, when driving in the country, he saw a barn. It was similar to his father's barn just outside of Regina, Saskatchewan. As he drove past, he remembered the time he and his pals got caught smoking behind the barn. He said he broke into a laugh and promptly grabbed his tape recorder and recorded the smoking incident. At the same time, he recorded other farm-related stories that came to mind.

He hopes to leave his son as detailed a picture of the past as possible. He contacted several relatives to fill in some of the blanks. He then researched his roots using websites and genealogical societies. His online detective work yielded a significant amount of information, and the cost, other than his time, was little or nothing.

What is going to be the gift you give to your family? Here are some things you may wish to consider as a living memories for your loved ones:

- A listing and description of your values and beliefs
- Things learned from grandparents, parents, children, spouse, and others
- What you are grateful for
- Hopes for the future
- Important events in your life and the lives of your relatives
- Things you regret not doing
- Your happiest times
- Lessons learned the hard way
- The importance of religion and spirituality

EXERCISE 19

Begin a genealogical record of your family:

1. Write down as much as you know about you and your parents, sisters, brothers, aunts, uncles, cousins, grandparents, and other family members. List names, years and places of birth, occupations, education, places of residence, year of death, known illnesses, and accomplishments.

2. Visit one or more genealogical websites to enter your family information and begin your genealogy search.

3. Contact relatives to obtain an oral and written record of your family members.

4. Organize your family information in a format that can be gifted to your loved ones (e.g., tapes, notebook, scrapbook, etc.)

Notes for getting started on your gift to your family:

_____

_____

_____

_____

_____

_____

EXERCISE 20

Imagine Your Legacy

Goals	By
Find a way to support local parks.	*2020*

_____

_____

_____

_____

_____

_____

_____

_____

Chapter 12

Put Things in Writing

Summary:

We live in a fast-paced world with tremendous convenience, and we love to get things done quickly. We rush around, moving from one project to the next with little or no time to think about what we have done and how we did it. However, if we are to be successful in our retirement life, we need to take time to reflect on our actions to see what worked, consider what we could have done differently, and plan for our next challenges. The simple act of writing is a way to slow down and assess where we've been and where we are going.

Sally and Thelma talk about the importance of keeping a written record of retirement planning.

In this chapter, there is an example of a journal entry and an exercise about journal writing.

As Thelma and Sally were preparing to leave Chuck's, Thelma said, "Sally, I'm glad to hear you're making notes about your thoughts, plans, and actions regarding your retirement planning. The successful retirees I know all stress the importance of having some sort of written record — a documentation of their retirement plan, actions taken, thoughts, perspectives, and observations. It's the written details of their journey through life and into retirement and their progress into a new way of living.

"Writing can also be an effective way to manage stress and enhance personal growth. It's easy to do and provides an opportunity to record dreams, purpose in life, memories, and feelings — what's important to you now and what you are grateful for.

"Along with your goals, milestones, and action plans, I suggest you record what worked or is working, what didn't, your successes, and the challenges. Note how you are doing with your retirement compared to others as well as your thoughts, feelings, and comments about how your retirement is unfolding."

An example of a journal entry could be:

Today, I had a conversation with William, who retired at the same time I did. He is still struggling with his retirement plan and has no well-thought-out direction. He keeps referring back to his old job and buddies. In thinking about William, I am happy with the progress I am making. I have a vision, plan, and action steps. Currently, I am searching for a mentor to help finalize my thinking. I regularly talk to my partner about our life ahead and very seldom look back. I have not forgotten my past, but I am moving forward. I feel sorry for William and am hopeful I can help him.

Some of the things I need to address in the coming days and weeks are re-evaluating my circle of friends and how I can enlarge my social circle. I need to make an appointment with my financial advisor, and I need to review my will. I want to have my financial plans completed by month's end and my will redrafted within three weeks. I am feeling physically and emotionally well and am very

much looking forward to the coming challenges and ad-
ventures retirement presents.

One fear I have is failing in my retirement plans. To help
me over my fear, I plan to meet with my mentors at least
once a month to discuss steps that will help keep me on
track.

"You're right, Thelma," said Sally. "At first, I found writing my thoughts and plans awkward and time-consuming, but now, as I get into the writing habit, it's actually fun to jot down my musings, and I enjoy reading my journal entries from the previous seven days. In this way, I'm able to see the progress or lack of progress I'm making towards my retirement goals. I'm highlighting my areas of success and the reasons for it as well as areas I need to work on. This helps me with planning for the coming week."

"If you ever want my critique on what you've written, whether it's your retirement plan, how you want to be remembered, or anything else, please don't hesitate to ask."

As Sally was putting on her coat to leave Chuck's, she turned to Thelma and said, "Thanks, Thelma. I appreciate your offer. Also, thanks for your time today. By the way, Chuck's pumpkin spice lattes are really good. See you soon."

Together, Sally and Thelma walked to the door, hugged, and said goodbye.

EXERCISE 21

As a practice entry in your journal, write a few lines out-lining why you are looking forward to retirement and the things you wish to explore and accomplish.

1. I am looking forward to retirement because...

_____
_____
_____
_____
_____
_____
_____
_____

2. The things I want to explore and accomplish when re-tired are...

_____
_____
_____
_____
_____
_____
_____
_____

Chapter 13

Dealing with Fear and Increasing Self-Confidence

Summary:

Retirement is a time of great change. The adoption of a new lifestyle, being more self-reliant, making decisions on health and well-being, and taking on new and different responsibilities increase the chances for fears to grow. Fears such as:

- Will I lose my physical or mental health as I age?
- Will I have sufficient monies to accomplish my retirement plans?
- Will disputes or mood swings affect my relationship with my spouse and friends?
- As a retiree, will I get the recognition I feel I deserve?

Fears and non-assertiveness cause feelings of unease. If not addressed, they can become obstacles between you and a happy retirement.

Sally and Vivian, her hairstylist, talk about fears and how best to deal with them. They also discuss how best to maintain and improve one's level of confidence and assertiveness.

In this chapter are two case studies and two exercises.

Three days after meeting with Thelma, Sally was seated in her local beauty parlour, reading an article on the increase of fear in people approaching retirement. Before she could finish the article, her hairstylist, Vivian, came over to complete the highlights Sally had requested.

"Vivian," said Sally, "you seem to be a fairly fearless person. You immigrated to this country ten years ago, learned English, raised two children on your own, and bought a twenty-five percent share of this parlour. What makes you unafraid to take risks?"

"That's an interesting question," said Vivian. "I think a big part of my willingness to venture into unknown waters is my positiveness. I keep reminding myself how fortunate I am to have my health, a loving family, and friends and to live in a free country.

"I know my strengths and ability to adapt to change. I think about the changes I've already managed success-fully, including facing life as a divorcee, finding my way to this country, learning a new language, raising my two children, and buying into this business. When I do fail, like the time I bought a used car that turned out to be a clunker, I remind myself that if I didn't make mistakes, I would never learn how to improve. That used car fiasco made me do my homework when I bought my current car, which, by the way, is one of my best purchases."

"Are there any other words of wisdom you have about dealing with fears?" asked Sally.

"Yes, when I'm afraid of something, I find it helps to talk to others about what's bothering me and to hear their perspectives. This, I find, helps me understand my fear and oftentimes gives me new ideas on how to handle the situation. For instance, when I was thinking about buying into this salon, I met with my financial advisor and banker about my fear, and together we planned how to make my investment a reality without endangering my retirement portfolio. Why do you ask?"

What to do when facing a fear:
- Stay positive
- Acknowledge your strengths and ability to adapt to change
- Take responsibility for your mistakes
- Share your fears with people you love and respect
- Collaborate on important issues
- Focus on your retirement plan

Remember, retirement is a time of change that will continue in one form or another for the rest of your life. It's part of life, and you need to deal with it. It's also one of the most exciting times: a time for exploration, a shift in focus, and a constant demand for new knowledge and skills. This includes finding ways to react constructively to your fears. Don't let yourself grow numb to possibilities but rather take responsibility for yourself and your situation and address your fears.

Sally replied, "Recently, I was informed I'm losing my job at Benson & Sons because of cutbacks. After the shock, I've been considering semi-retirement. This has opened a huge Pandora's box of things to think about, including what I would do with my time, whether I will have enough money, how best do I maintain my health, where to live, what my social circle will be, and the list goes on. In the past weeks, I've met with several people, including my friend Thelma, who have been great in providing me with insights and information. My planning is taking shape, and I'm getting excited about the rest of my life. However, there are times, especially when I'm alone, when I feel afraid of all this change."

"I'm so sorry to hear about your job loss. In the past, when you've talked about your job and company, I could tell how much you loved what you do. You were always enthusiastic about work, and it meant a lot to you. If there is anything I can do as you transition to something new, please don't hesitate to ask.

"As for dealing with fear, I've found talking with good friends and family goes a long way to mitigate my fear. I certainly don't want my fear to grow so it stops me from progressing to my goals. I also remind myself that my fears help to protect me. For instance, my fear of being involved in a car crash makes me drive within the speed limit, wear a seatbelt, and watch out for careless drivers. My fear of falling makes me take extra precautions when walking down stairs or when walking on ice."

"That's an interesting way to look at fear. I've never thought about that way. Thanks for that."

"What you're doing, getting advice and ideas from friends and others, sounds very adult, and I congratulate you on your initiative."

Paul retired two years ago at the age of sixty-five. Though he was in good health, he was afraid he would not enjoy a healthy retirement, as his father had died of heart disease in his sixties. Paul also feared that he and his wife, Celia, could experience difficulty with their relationship because they have led fairly separate lives.

To address his fears, Paul listed the reasons for his

health concerns and made an appointment with his doctor. This resulted in a full physical examination, including a visit with a cardiologist.

Paul received a clean bill of health, which went a long way to alleviate his concerns. He and Celia talked about their privacy needs and together drafted a plan for spending time together. Paul is now feeling much more at ease, and his retirement fears have abated.

EXERCISE 22

List your fears about retirement	Actions you plan to take
Being valued	*Helping the less fortunate*
Spending time alone	*Meeting buddies for coffee*

_____

_____

_____

_____

_____

_____

_____

"Thank you so much, Vivian. I appreciate your support," said Sally. "But I have a question. What's the difference between fear and confidence?"

"Fear and confidence may be considered opposites. Fear is a negative emotion, but confidence is a positive one. For instance, fear often happens when you want to escape a situation, whereas confidence urges you to jump into the situation with an anticipation of solving the problem. Though self-confidence is important at every age, I believe its importance increases as we grow older. A confident person stands up for what they believe in, expresses feelings honestly, and does it without trampling on the rights of others."

"I can see where self-confidence is needed in retirement. Just last week I was in a restaurant and was appalled by the service. Not only did I not complain, but I also left a tip. When I was walking out, I felt ashamed for not saying anything. What do you suggest I do to increase my confidence?"

"I've experienced the same feeling of shame and disappointment myself. I've done some research on self-confidence and how debilitating it can be when you can't assert yourself. For instance, if I'm not satisfied with a restaurant meal, I call the waiter over and quietly give a specific reason for my dissatisfaction, like, 'My meal is cold,' or 'My meat was not cooked as ordered.' In most instances, the waiter or waitress acts on my complaint without any further ado. However, if the waiter doesn't take action, I ask to speak with the chef or maître d'. If they don't respond, I make my dissatisfaction clear in a loud voice, loud enough for surrounding diners to hear. Then I take my coat and walk out! It's a wonderful feeling staying in control and not letting the situation control you.

"Let's practice," suggested Vivian. "Let's say you're interested in having a couple of rooms in your house painted. What would the confident Sally do to ensure good service?"

Sally thought for a moment and then said, "Well, I'd get estimates from at least two paint contractors and then ensure, when hiring a contractor, to have my wants clearly recorded and agreed to before the work begins. Then, as soon as I realize there is a problem, I would contact the contractor and tell them what the problem is. I'd stay calm and make sure to hold the conversation in private to minimize any embarrassment in front of other tradespeople.

If they redo the work to my satisfaction, I'd thank the contractor. But if they don't complete it to my satisfaction, I'd hold back payment until I was satisfied."

"Bravo, Sally, good answer! Just as a learning point, in any assertive situation, it's important to stay calm, listen to the other party, and suggest alternatives so that both parties feel satisfied. The moment you get angry, fearful, or belligerent, you lose. If the other party gets angry, either absorb their comments or deflect them, but do not respond in kind. After each situation, ask yourself, 'What am I proud about in how I handled this situation?' 'What am I not proud about?' 'What will I do differently next time?' Each time you ask these questions, you hone your confidence skills to the point where being assertive in tough situations will come naturally."

"Thank you for all your advice today. I want to be a confident and assertive person in retirement and not a person who feels helpless."

"I see you as an in-control retiree who does well in mastering the challenges retirement throws your way."

"Thanks, Vivian, for your vote of confidence. By the way, I love what you did with my hair today. I'll see you again in about two months. Goodbye."

Willard is fifty-nine years old and a successful manager with a large electronics company. Though confident at work, he has difficulty being assertive with tradespeople, gas station attendants, store clerks, waiters, and others outside his job. He is used to accepting poor service without saying anything. Though he'd get furious on the inside, he'd do nothing outwardly.

One day, a friend commented on Willard's non-assertive behaviour and suggested he assert himself. His friend demonstrated how to ask for what is wanted and convinced Willard he would feel better about himself.

Willard's first test of his newly acquired confidence came when he asked for a lower interest rate on a credit card. He approached his bank manager and stated his request without threats of taking his business elsewhere. In return, the manager invited him into his office, opened his computer to Willard's accounts, and thanked him for his continued business.

The manager studied the interest rate currently being charged and then said, "Based on your credit rating, it would be my pleasure to adjust your interest rate by one and a half basis points. Would that meet your satisfaction?"

Willard was delighted. After shaking hands with the manager, he walked out of the office with a feeling of satisfaction and pride resulting from his assertive action.

EXERCISE 23

Take a moment to think about yourself. Are you naturally assertive, non-assertive, or aggressive? What were the factors that led to your assertiveness, non-assertiveness, or aggressiveness?

_____

_____

_____

_____

_____

_____

_____

_____

What can you do to improve your assertiveness (e.g., calmly repeat what you want over and over like a broken record, let criticism roll off your back, stand up for your rights, etc.)?

_____

_____

_____

_____

_____

_____

_____

_____

Chapter 14

How to Have Fun

Summary:

Laughter is the best medicine. Laughing and having fun helps us relax. When we laugh, our body produces endorphins that help cellular development and create a feeling of well-being.

As a successful retiree, look at your world and ask how you can add more fun into your life.

Sally asks Thelma for ideas on how to have fun

In this chapter is a list of thirty-one ways to have fun and a fun exercise.

As Sally was sitting at her dining room table, thinking of her balanced leisure lifestyle plan, she thought, "How can I add more fun into my life? What are the whimsical and amusing things I can do to add fun and excitement to my life?" With these questions swirling in her mind, she picked up her phone and called Thelma.

"Hi, Thelma, it's Sally. I have a quick question. What do you do to have fun?"

"Interesting question. As a librarian, I live in a world of books and, for the most part, serious conversation. I've known fellow workers who take themselves too seriously, so I infuse fun things into my regular routine.

"One thing I do for fun is transform my dining room into a blanket fort when my two six-year-old nieces come to visit. I drape a sheet over the table and pile cushions under and around the table. We have a wonderful time, including having our lunch in the fort.

"Another fun thing is giving a sincere thank you to store clerks, gas station attendants, and supermarket cashiers. I'm always amazed at their facial expressions and replies. For most of them, this is a highlight of their day.

"What things can you see yourself doing to add joy to your days?" asked Thelma.

"I'd like to buy several stuffed animals and give them to a local seniors' home. When distributing the toys, I would take the time to talk to the seniors and find out something interesting about each person. Another idea is to volunteer for the next Santa Claus parade. I remember watching the parade with my children."

"Those are good ideas. Obviously, you can go out and buy entertainment, but I like to do easy, affordable things to have some fun in everyday life."

Have Fun Outside

1. Have a picnic in the park and ask everyone to make something from scratch.
2. Make your own kite, then head to the beach to fly it.
3. Download a map app for your iPhone and bike and explore a new area.
4. Have a nostalgia hunt at a flea market. Look for G.I. Joes, My Little Pony, Cabbage Patch Kids, or anything else you loved as a kid.
5. Go geocaching, an outdoor activity where treasure hunters use GPS or mobile devices to hide and seek items around the world.

Have Fun with Food

1. Swap family recipes with a friend and make each other's dishes to enjoy together.
2. Have a cookie swap party. Everyone makes a dozen and goes home with a dozen of all different types of cookies.
3. Take turns hosting dinners with friends. It's much less expensive than going out to eat, and it gives everyone a turn to host.
4. Start your own *Julie & Julia* project. Grab a cookbook, start working your way through it, and blog about it as you go.

Have Fun with Entertainment

1. Have a karaoke night using a YouTube karaoke channel
2. Look on Craigslist for your area to see if there are any free concerts going on in nearby parks.
3. Have a movie marathon with one or two friends where everyone brings their favourite DVD.
4. Spend a day looking for free street performances in the nearest big city. There are usually many going on in the summer.
5. Have a culture day. Visit a museum on a free day, listen to classical music on the way, and watch a classic movie in the evening.
6. Call your local theatre to see if they take volunteer ushers. Many theatres give free tickets to volunteers who either seat guests or clean up post-performance.
7. If you have children, host a family barbecue where the adults catch up while the kids come up with a little show to perform later in the evening. (My favourite childhood memories all involve a show with the cousins!)
8. Use Facebook to get a group together for a flash

mob. You'll need a lot of people — and undoubtedly, this requires work — but it can be a ton of fun to prepare and carry out.

Have Fun by Trading

1. Host a clothes swap day where everyone brings clothing and accessories they no longer want and everyone goes home with something new. (This may be more for the ladies.)
2. Trade books with a friend and then get together to discuss the most insightful, helpful, or entertaining parts.
3. Have a board game night where everyone brings their favourite game. (Okay, so this is more sharing than trading.)
4. Trade your services for someone else's. Offer to help your painter friend set up a website in exchange for painting your bedroom. It will be a fun, free, productive afternoon.
5. Have a no-money garage sale on a sunny afternoon. List on Craigslist everything you have that you'd like to get rid of and include a list of everything you want in exchange.
6. Trade videos with a loved one who lives far away. Each of you plan a day of fun without telling each other what it will entail. Then go through the day with the intention of creating a joy-filled video to send later that evening.
7. Trade blogs. You host your friend's blog for a day and let him or her host yours. If you both write about different subjects, this is an incentive to try writing something new.

Have Fun by Giving Back

1. Host a free webinar sharing something that you're passionate about.

2. Sign up to be a volunteer dog walker through the SPCA and Humane Society. (You can also help organize fundraising events, provide general animal care, and assist with grooming, among other things.)

3. Call your local children's hospital and see if you can host a sing-a-long or come dressed up as a clown to spread cheer. (Contributor Harriet Cabelly did something similiar through Gesundheit Global Outreach clowning trips.)

4. Volunteer to help with events at your local zoo. Some zoos require an extensive time commitment, but others take short-term volunteers for specific events.

5. Be an unofficial park volunteer for a day. In between relaxing and reading books on the grass, pick up litter to keep the area clean.

6. Use Charity Navigator to find a local charity that you like and then get involved in volunteering today.

7. Help an elderly neighbour with her garden or with another chore that you generally enjoy doing.

"The next time we meet, let's share our fun ideas for activities," Sally suggested.

"Great idea," said Thelma.

"See you soon."

EXERCISE 24

List some ways you and your partner can have fun. Be imaginative.

_____

_____

_____

_____

_____

_____

_____

_____

Chapter 15

Death and Dying

You don't get to choose how you're going to die. Or when. You can only decide how you're going to live. Now.
— Joan Baez

Summary:

We all like to imagine retirement as a time we will enjoy to the fullest by doing whatever it is we want to do. Although this is true, it is also a time when we could face the death of a loved one.

People deal with death in different ways. Regardless of your methods, you will likely need some help coping during your time of loss.

After learning of a cousin's death, Sally talks to Thelma about the stages of grieving.

This chapter includes a case study.

Sally called Thelma with news.

"Thelma, I just received a phone call saying my cousin Bart died while skiing. He was only fifty-four. He hit a tree while skiing in Whistler, BC."

"I'm so sorry to hear of your loss. Were you and Bart close?"

"Yes," sobbed Sally. "He and I went to school together, and his family and mine used to go to the beach, have barbeques, and celebrate the holidays together. Bart was more of a brother than a cousin. I can't believe he's gone. I'm having trouble believing he's dead."

"You've just had a huge shock. I'm here for you. How are you feeling? Do you want to meet at Chuck's?"

"Thank you. I haven't experienced many deaths in my life. My mind is a roller coaster of emotions right now."

"For some people," Thelma explained, "they deny the news, then become angry about a passing, especially if it's a spouse or partner. Thoughts such as, 'How could John die? We were both looking forward to our retirement and spending time with each other, travelling, remodelling our home, and now he's gone!' This anger is common and natural and helps us move towards regaining control of life.

"Another stage of grieving is bargaining. When we ask the 'what if' questions like, 'What would have happened if I had done more for him?' or 'What if I had been more supportive?' Some people beat themselves up about the past. What's done is done, and it cannot be changed.

"After the bargaining stage, there is normally a resignation of the person's passing. In this stage, you start to accept reality. You begin to get balance back in your life and you can start looking forward. Obviously, there will still be lows, but they will be more in balance with the highs.

"Then finally," said Thelma, "is acceptance. You truly accept the passing of your loved one. You begin to review your options and make decisions about the rest of your life. Throughout your grieving process, it's important to keep in touch with friends and family, including, I hope, with me. Please remember I'm here for you. Anytime you feel like talking, call me."

"Thank you so much," said Sally. "You are a good friend and I appreciate your caring."

"Don't forget to speak with your doctor if you feel your grief is affecting your health," said Thelma. "There are support groups and agencies that can be helpful. When a friend of mine lost his wife, his family was extremely supportive, but he knew he needed additional support. The Canadian Mental Health Association helped find him the support."

"Thank you, Thelma. I feel a bit better just sharing my news with you and hearing your support. Bye for now."

Janice recently lost her husband, Herb. He had not been well for the last six months, and though the doctors were optimistic about his recovery, Janice thought the worst.

When Herb eventually died, Janice's immediate reaction was denial. He was always there, and he would return. She then became angry, not only at Herb for leaving her alone in retirement but also at herself for being reliant on him. He'd been the one who paid the bills, did the banking, and dealt with their financial advisor, all the things she now had to do.

As part of her grieving, Janice began thinking Herb would have lived longer if only she had made him see his doctor when he started to complain about his ailments. She also thought he would have survived longer if she was a better wife.

Janice then became resigned to Herb's passing, and she began to pick up the pieces. She paid the bills, closed Herb's bank account, met with the financial advisor, contacted a support group for widows, and met with her reli-

gious leader about volunteering. She was moving on.

Throughout her grieving, Janice's friends Alicia, Marcia, and Joanne were with her every step of the way. They shared frequent phone calls, met for lunch, went on walks, or just sat and talked. Her friends were her anchors as she navigated the stormy seas of grief.

Chapter 16

Making a Will

Summary:

Many people die each year without a will. According to a recent AARP survey, two out of five adults over forty-five years of age do not have a will.

If you die without a will, the province or state in which you live will decide how to distribute your estate. Based on impersonal formulas for the distribution of assets, some money or belongings may not end up with the beneficiaries as intended.

Sally meets with Emmanuel John, a lawyer specializing in wills, accompanying letters, and estate and advance care planning.

This chapter includes a case study and an exercise.

Two weeks after the funeral of her cousin Bart, Sally asked Thelma if she could recommend a lawyer to help her prepare her will.

"Bart died without a will," Sally said. "I don't want that to happen with me. I wouldn't forgive myself for causing such chaos for my family, especially for my children."

"I'd recommend you talk to Emmanuel Johns," Thelma said. "I met him when my mother was ill, and he helped both Mom and me prepare our respective wills. I greatly appreciated his patience and understanding regarding our needs and wants. Do you wish me to call him?"

"That would be helpful. Thanks. What are the highlights I should keep in mind?"

"Whatever you do, I strongly recommend using the services of a lawyer. I've talked to many people who tried creating a will themselves using forms they found on the Internet, much to their horror. But it's okay to map out what your estate consists of and how you want it divided before you see a lawyer. This will help you sort out your options and probably save you time and money.

"When I met with Emmanuel, he suggested preparing a letter to accompany my will in which I list people and institutions to be notified of my death. For instance, I'd really like my Aunt Maud and Uncle Frank to be called. They now live in Australia, but when I was growing up, I spent many weekends with them. They are kind, and I love them to bits. In my letter, I've listed their names, address, and telephone number but also others to be contacted. I hope my list will make it easier for the person assuming the responsibility for calling.

"Other items listed in my accompanying letter are my funeral arrangements and last wishes. Some of my wishes are to have a simple casket and have 'Over the Rainbow' from the *The Wizard of Oz* play during the service. Who would know it's my favourite song?

"Then, of course, there is the listing of my bank accounts and bank locations, credit cards, mortgage papers, insurance policies, and investments. I've also listed my assets and the names of those to whom the articles are to be given.

"It's amazing what a relief it is once you have your will and accompanying letter completed. I let two family members know where my will and letter are stored and the name and address of my lawyer, Emmanuel."

Gabrielle does not want to burden her family with undue hardship when she passes on. She wants to make the settlement of her affairs as easy as possible. She updates her will every three years, at which time she reviews and modifies the comments of her accompanying letter. She also provides a best friend with a copy of her will and accompanying letter.

Though Gabrielle isn't planning to leave this earth anytime soon, she has the peace of mind that her last wishes will be followed. She also knows her family and friends will not be put through the anguish of trying to locate her personal papers and documents at a time that will be difficult enough.

A week later, Sally met with Emmanuel Johns, the lawyer Thelma and her mother had used to help prepare their wills. Emmanuel's office was downtown, a quick subway ride for Sally.

"Welcome. It's a pleasure to meet you, Sally. Thelma speaks highly of you. How can I help?" said Emmanuel.

"I need to prepare my will and an accompanying letter. I must admit I've not heard of such a letter, but when Thelma mentioned it, the letter makes sense."

A will is a legal document which says who will manage your estate after you die. Your estate iseverything you own. The person who manages your estate is the executor.

A will can also say who will become the guardian for any

minor children, and who you want to receive specific items you own. Someone who receives any of your property is a beneficiary.

Emmanuel said, "I recommend preparing such a letter to all my clients. Such a document eases the burden for not only the executor but also the family. It spells out your wishes and helps ensure a constructive settling of your estate."

"What happens if I die without a will?" asked Sally. "My cousin just died in an accident, and he didn't have a will."

"If you die without a valid will, you'll become what's called intestate. That usually means your estate will be settled based on the laws of the province or state you lived in. A will outlines who inherits what. Probate is the legal process of transferring the property of a deceased person to the rightful heirs.

"If no executor is named, a judge appoints an administrator to serve in that capacity. An administrator also will be named if a will is deemed to be invalid. All wills must meet certain standards such as being witnessed to be legally valid. Again, requirements vary from province to province.

"An administrator will most likely be a stranger to you and your family, and they will be bound by the letter of the probate laws of your province. As such, an administrator may make decisions that wouldn't necessarily agree with your wishes or those of your heirs.

"Let me ask you, Sally. Do you have someone in mind to act as your executor?"

The normal responsibilities of an executor include:

- Locating your original will and documents amending your will
- Confirming with your lawyer that your will is valid
- Securing inventories and appraising your valuables and assets
- Participating in your funeral arrangements and, if necessary, notifying your next of kin
- Protecting your property, including the continuation of fire and theft coverage
- Hiring a lawyer to obtain probate, if necessary
- Identifying debts and paying all bills, taxes, and creditors
- Getting investment, legal, business, and tax advice
- Distributing your assets to your beneficiaries according to your wishes
- Filing final tax returns of the estate
- Accounting for the administration of the estate

"I'm thinking of asking my niece Francisca," Sally said. "She lives here in the city and has always had my best interests in mind. As a backup, there is my eldest son, Jerry."

"Good," said Emmanuel. "It's surprising the number of clients who have not considered the need of a backup executor. Your son Jerry would take the place of your niece Francisca if for some reason she is unable to fulfill her duties. I suggest, after today's meeting, you contact your niece and son and get their consent. Normally, family members are motivated to work quickly, and most do so without a fee. By law, executors are entitled to be paid up to five percent of your estate for their time and effort. Do you have a business, substantial investments, or rental properties? If so, you may need an executor with special skills."

"No, I don't," said Sally.

"Before we get started drafting your will, do you have any questions?" asked Emmanuel.

"I don't want to sound rude, but do I need a lawyer to prepare my will?"

"No, you aren't required to hire a lawyer to prepare your will, though an experienced lawyer can provide useful advice on estate planning strategies such as living trusts. But as long as your will meets the legal requirements of your province, it's valid whether a lawyer drafted it or you wrote it yourself on the back of a napkin."

"Thelma was adamant I should use a lawyer."

"Yes, I understand. I shared with Thelma situations where people created their will using online guides only to find out they missed a crucial element, resulting in the will getting tangled up in court and long delays before any money could be dispersed to the family. A good lawyer will prevent such traps, plus ensure you consider essential estate planning documents and advance planning such as financial and healthcare powers of attorney to ensure your wishes are carried out while you're still alive."

"If I ever meet a significant other in the future, should my partner and I have a joint will or separate wills?"

"Estate planners almost universally advise against joint wills, and some jurisdictions don't even recognize them. Odds are you and your partner won't die at the same time, and there will probably be property that's not jointly held. That's why separate wills make better sense, even though your will and your partner's will might end up looking remarkably similar.

"In particular, separate wills allow for each partner to

address issues such as ex-spouses and children from previous relationships. Same thing for property obtained during a previous marriage. You have to be very clear about who gets what. And probate laws generally favour the current partner."

"Who should act as a witness to a will?"

"Any person can act as a witness to your will, but you should select someone who isn't a beneficiary. Otherwise there's the potential for a conflict of interest. The technical term is a disinterested witness. Some provinces require two or more witnesses. If a lawyer drafts your will, they shouldn't serve as a witness.

"Not all provinces require a will to be notarized, but some do. Witnesses should sign what's called a self-proving affidavit in the presence of a notary. This affidavit can speed up the probate process because your witnesses likely won't be called into court by a judge to validate their signatures and the authenticity of the will."

"Where should I keep my will?"

"A probate court usually requires your original will before it can process your estate, so it's important to keep the document safe yet accessible. If you put the will in a bank safe deposit box that only you can get into, your family might need to seek a court order to gain access. A waterproof and fireproof safe in your house is a good alternative.

"If you use me to create your will, our office will keep copies in case the original is destroyed. Signed copies can be used to establish your intentions. However, the absence of an original will can complicate matters, and without it, there's no guarantee that your estate will be settled as you'd hoped."

"How often does a will need to be updated?"

"It's possible that your will may never need to be updated — or you may choose to update it regularly. The decision is yours. Remember, the only version of your will that matters is the most current valid one in existence at the time of your death.

"With that in mind, you may want to revisit your will at times of major life changes. Think of pivotal moments such as marriage, divorce, the birth of a child, the death of a beneficiary or executor, a significant purchase or inheritance, and so on. Your kids probably won't need guardians named in a will after they're adults, for example, but you might still need to name guardians for disabled dependents. A rule of thumb: Review your will every two or three years to be safe."

"One more question," said Sally. "Who has the right to contest my will?"

"Contesting a will refers to challenging the legal validity of all or part of the document. A beneficiary who feels slighted by the terms of a will might choose to contest it. A spouse, ex-spouse, or child might believe your stated wishes go against local probate laws, depending on which province you live in.

"A will can be contested for any number of other reasons: it wasn't properly witnessed; you weren't competent when you signed it; or it's the result of coercion or fraud. It's usually up to a probate judge to settle the dispute. The key to successfully contesting a will is finding legitimate legal fault with it. A clearly drafted and validly executed will is the best defense.

"Would you like to begin?" asked Emmanuel.

"Yes, I certainly would. Thank you for answering my questions," said Sally.

EXERCISE 25

In the following space or on a separate piece of paper:

1. Name your executor and the reasons for your choice.

_____

_____

_____

_____

_____

_____

_____

_____

2. Prepare your accompanying letter beginning with a list of people to be notified when you die.

_____

_____

_____

_____

_____

_____

_____

3. If you have been married more than once, what special consideration would you make regarding your ex-spouse and your children from those marriages?

_____

_____

_____

_____

_____

_____

_____

_____

4. If you are in a committed but unmarried union, what have you and your partner done to protect each other legally? What more should you do?

_____

_____

_____

_____

_____

_____

_____

"Sally, once your will is created, there is another matter I'd suggest you consider," said Emmanuel.

"What's that?" asked Sally.

"To draft an advance care plan — a document outlining your wishes for care at the end of life. It's surprising how many people don't have such a plan and have never had a conversation with loved ones about what is important to them. For instance, do you prefer to die at home, in a hospice, or in the hospital? Do you want or not want certain medical interventions such as resuscitation or feeding tubes if it's unlikely you would survive or live independently? Who will make medical decisions on your behalf should you become incapable of doing so?"

"When is an advance care plan used?" asked Sally.

"Your plan is used only if you are mentally incapable of making your own healthcare decisions — for instance, if you are in a coma or your illness has impaired your ability to communicate your decisions. Your substitute decision maker or makers can use your plan to guide your care, advocate for your wishes, and consent or refuse consent to treatment on your behalf."

"My family will know what to do. Why do I have to write it down?"

"Writing down your wishes helps to ensure your wishes are clear for everyone. You may believe that they know what to do, but they may not. For example, you may have said something like 'pull the plug if I'm a vegetable,' but you need to be clear about what that really means to you. Your family may also have questions about the wishes you have made. Writing down those wishes may help the conversation."

"Thanks for suggesting we put together an advance care plan. I see why it's important to have a plan like that. I've now got some homework to do before we meet again. Emmanuel, would you be available to meet with me in, say, two weeks?"

"Let me see. How about the twenty-fifth at ten in the morning? Does that work for you?"

"Perfect. I'll see you then. Thank you for your time today and your valuable information and insights."

Chapter 17

Finding and Using a Retirement Mentor

Summary:

With many people retiring earlier, being retired for ten to thirty or more years may become common. That's a long time. As part of your retirement preparation, consider finding and using one or more mentors to provide you with the advice and emotional support you need to be a successful retiree.

Thelma and Sally recognize the importance of a retirement mentor.

In this chapter are tips on how to find and use a retirement mentor. Also in this chapter are a case study and an exercise about mentors.

As Thelma and Sally settled into their favourite stuffed chairs at Chuck's, Sally said, "I appreciate all the time and care you've given me with my life planning. The more we talk, the more comfortable I am about accepting retirement as the best course of action. I'm not sure how I can repay you for what you've done."

"It's been fun," said Thelma. "Throughout our discussions, we've, I believe, formed a stronger bond and enriched our friendship. It has been gratifying to see you succeed and grow; this has given me a great sense of pride. When we first started our conversations, I wondered how much time and energy it was going to take. Now I'm pleased we started on this journey, and I really look forward to continuing our coffee time at Chuck's.

"I'm amazed by the number of people who enter retirement without any help. When you think about it, as we matured, we worked, raised a family, and had many mentors along the way — our parents, family members, teachers, friends, coaches, business associates, supervisors, and managers. They all showed us the way, pointing out the pitfalls in life and helping steer us around the traps. They encouraged and praised us, and they helped guide our actions. Retirement is filled with adventure, change, and the unknown. Faced with this new part of life, we each have a choice: to jump into retirement with both feet, without any planning or discussion or to enter retirement fully prepared.

"I'm pleased to have been your mentor. You appreciated my assistance, were willing to risk trying ideas and approaches I suggested, and welcomed the people I introduced you to, and we were able to share our interests and understandings."

Here are some steps you can take to finding a suitable mentor:

1. Acknowledge that it is hard to have a great retirement without help. One or more mentors can assist you in developing your retirement vision and plan. They can play the devil's advocate to help hone your thinking. They can also provide you with ideas and options designed to achieve your retirement goals.

2. Ask yourself if there are one or two people in your imme-

diate family who can serve as your mentor. You can consider a work colleague or friend, someone who already has created a successful retirement plan, or someone who is already a retiree that you admire. Ask yourself: Why do I consider this person to be a good potential mentor? What is it about them I respect and would be appreciative of regarding any assistance and guidance?

3. Ask yourself: What would make me an attractive mentee to my potential mentor? Do I have the desire and ability to accept advice and guidance from this person? Do I possess a positive attitude towards retirement? Would I be appreciative of assistance and willing to risk trying ideas and approaches suggested by this person? Will I be comfortable disclosing personal stories and feelings to this person? Would we be able to share interests as part of the relationship building process?

4. Once you identify one or more potential mentors, meet with them individually to discuss the potential of establishing a mentor/mentee relationship. It may be as simple as meeting once a month or two to generally discuss your retirement progress or it may be as complex as scheduling weekly or biweekly critiques of your retirement plan and actions.

When Donnie was approaching retirement at age sixty-three, he knew he would benefit from having a mentor. He thought about those he knew who were successfully retired and approached Ryan, a friend he respected and who had retired five years earlier. Donnie asked for his assistance with his retirement vision and plan and in the following months, they met regularly.

Ryan provided Donnie with insight and observations on all aspects of retirement, including how to build a dynamic health and wellness strategy, how to reinforce your relationship with your spouse, and what questions to ask a financial advisor.

Here are a few ways to help deepen your mentoring relationship:

- Develop an understanding of each other's background and issues
- Develop an environment of mutual admiration
- Treat each other as confidants
- Be open to your mentor's ideas and suggestions
- Help each other focus on resolvable problems
- Develop a relationship that is meaningful and valuable for both parties

Mentoring relationships are not to be entered into lightly. They require a commitment of time and energy by both the mentor and mentee if you wish to produce valuable, worthwhile results. With the proper mix of dedication and caution, mentoring can immensely enrich your retirement and your life.

EXERCISE 26

Think about a mentor who would be best suited to your current retirement needs. List your possible mentors.

_____

_____

_____

_____

_____

_____

_____

_____

List the most important benefits of a mentor to you.

_____

_____

_____

_____

_____

_____

_____

_____

As a mentee, how can you communicate your willingness to learn?
e.g., be open to my mentor's influence and ideas

_____

_____

_____

_____

_____

_____

_____

_____

How can you reward your mentor? Remember, your mentor is spending time assisting you.

_____

_____

_____

_____

_____

_____

_____

"Now, update me on your retirement vision and plan," said Thelma.

As Sally progressed with her retirement discussions with Thelma and others, she formulated a picture of what life may look like after leaving Benson & Sons. After each meeting, she noted the highlights of the talks and her own observations and feelings. From these insights, she had begun to see the direction her life would take.

Sally's New Role

No longer a marketing associate at Benson, Sally took a job as marketing representative for Stringer Sports, a start-up company specializing in tennis rackets and tennis apparel. When they interviewed her, the management team was impressed with her organizational skills and ability to relate to others. Her salary is half of what she made at Benson, but she participates in the firm's profit-sharing program. She works three days a week.

Sally volunteers with the local SPCA as a pet groomer and assistant rescuer of animals in distress. Though she has just begun volunteering, she has already found a new sense of purpose. She has met people with similar interests and has been invited to participate in several association events.

To ensure the welfare of her mother, Agnes, Sally visits the nursing home once a week. When there, she takes Agnes for walks, lunch, or to a local concert. Sally feels relieved and is appreciative of the time she and her mother have before Alzheimer's disease takes its toll.

Sally and her children, Jerry, Michael, and Emily, plan BBQs together and family nights. Sally's relationship with her children are changing from parent to friend, which is a comforting realization before they make their way in the world.

Balanced Leisure Lifestyle

Sally has developed a balanced leisure lifestyle. Though it's complete, she knows there will be experimentation and adjustment over time until she finds the right mix. She's also prepared to make adjustments as opportunities arise and when her interests change.

Entertainment

Sally attends concerts, attends plays, and watches her favourite TV shows, *The View* and *60 Minutes*.

Education

Sally enrolled in a night school French course. She's already studying the language using Babbel, a language learning app. She also has an account with Ancestry.com and plans to research her family's genealogy.

Travel

The Trafalgar travel agency has provided Sally with information on interesting tours designed for single adults. Currently, she is researching a tour of castles and monasteries in Portugal.

Exercise

With the consent of her doctor, Sally joined a fitness program for women. After the initial assessment, the program director developed an individual set of activities to increase both her cardiovascular health and muscle strength. After two weeks, she has noticed she has more energy and better sleep. This, coupled with a change of diet recommended by a nutritionist, is helping make Sally feel great.

Social Activities

Sally attended a couple of local Probus club meetings. She was impressed with the congeniality of the members and the list of activities offered. She is now a member of the club and is constantly meeting new people. She has gone out on two coffee dates with Reginald, a man she met through the club.

Hobbies

This is the one area that is challenging Sally. She has tried oil painting, photography, and making wine, but none of these has maintained her interest. Over the next several months, she plans to try other hobbies.

Finances

With the help of her financial advisor, Daniel, Sally is now feeling financially secure. She has sufficient funds from her investments and pension plus the earnings from her part-time job to adequately fund her retirement. She plans to begin collecting her government pension at age sixty-two. Her lawyer, Mark, was able to negotiate more money from Benson & Sons as part of her severance package. With that money she can renovate her home and take one major trip every second year.

Daniel helped Sally create a monthly personal and household budget and she is maintaining her spending in accordance to it. At a glance, she can easily determine what she can afford week to week. The benefit of these tools is an increased sense of financial security.

Sally had her home appraised, and though she doesn't plan to move, she is content her house will keep appreciating in value and its eventual sale will support a decision to move into assisted-living accommodation.

Well-Being

As mentioned, Sally now has an exercise regime and diet and nutrition plan. To keep her mind active, she works on crossword puzzles in her local paper every day and, when she has a spare moment, completes word games and brain teasers. She has rejoined her religious organization and attends weekly services.

She has a well-drafted will and accompanying letter. She also has an advance care plan, which she has shared with her children.

Mentoring

Sally continues to meet regularly with Thelma, and the two of them discuss their retirement plans — what they are doing, their successes and challenges, etc. They provide each other with insight, encouragement, and suggestions.

Their sessions have deepened the relationship. They understand each other's motivation, have mutual admiration, treat each other as confidants, and are open to each other's ideas and suggestions.

In total, Sally's retirement plan has provided her with a clear vision and direction for life after work. She's confident she will be successful making the transition from work to retirement. She now exudes a confidence and happiness.

Chapter 18

Examples of Retirement Planning

The Story of Megan and David

Three years before their intended retirement, Megan and David began asking whether they could transition into life after work. Though they were prudent savers, questions of money, lifestyle, health, and relationships began to surface.

One of Megan's concerns was David's lack of outside interests and friends. David was driven by his job, and he channelled all of his energy into being a manager at his work. Megan, on the other hand, enjoyed her job as a fitness instructor and was socially active volunteering with the local theatre group and regularly meeting with her girlfriends.

When initially discussing retirement, David said he was looking forward to retirement so he could spend more time with Megan, something he did not do throughout his working career. Deep down, Megan knew this was going to be a bone of contention, as she enjoyed her freedom and, through necessity, had built an independent lifestyle.

In their quest for direction, Megan and David began reading articles and books on retirement, including Rick Atkinson's book *Strategies for Retiring Right!* They talked to friends and family members about life after work and the lessons they had learned. They sought out two people they believed had retired successfully and asked for advice.

As a result, Megan and David created their vision of retirement and plans of action for making their vision a reality.

The following is Megan and David's plan for life after work:

- Confirmation from their financial advisor that their prudent money management will provide money well into their nineties. They prepared a revised net worth statement with their advisor, and they adjusted their investment strategy to reflect retirement in three years.

- Megan and David are keeping to their well-established budgeting and continue to have discussions about finances and maintaining their spending in accordance to their personal and household budgets.

- Discussions between Megan and David, with the assistance of a retirement coach, resulted in building a balanced leisure lifestyle:
    - Megan will continue with her volunteering and her regular girls' night out plus working part-time as a fitness instructor. She will continue with her knitting and needlecrafts and will devote time to learning Spanish, one of her lifelong desires.
    - David, with the assistance of an exercise coach, is now following an exercise regime. His goal is to enter local cross-country races beginning twelve months from now. He also has become a member of a men's Probus club and is vice-chair of the tours committee. He is using every opportunity to meet new people and has already expanded his so-

cial circle. He has also found photography as a hobby and joined a local photography group.

- ■ Together, Megan and David attend concerts and plays and have a date night every two weeks. They also prepare and eat dinner together without TV or checking their phones. They're rediscovering lines of communication. They are members of a book club and enjoy discussing the book of the week over a bottle of their favourite wine.

- Megan and David prefer to stay in their current home, which is mortgage-free. They are having a new kitchen installed and are renovating the bathrooms. These changes to their home will both beautify their surroundings and add to the eventual selling price.

- Megan and David each found a mentor. They also meet with a retirement coach every four months to review their progress and tweak their individual retirement plans. As they succeed in retirement, they also plan, when approached, to be someone's mentors so they can pass on their retirement insights and experience.

The Retirement of Elma and Susan

Elma plans to retire in 2021. Susan, who is eight years younger than Elma, plans to continue working for another ten years.

Though they both are indifferent to life after work, they attended a retirement workshop. As a result, they came to the realization that retirement was creeping up quickly and they needed to begin their planning if they are to be successful retirees.

Financially, Elma and Susan are reasonably secure when they factor in their company pensions — Elma is a community leader and Susan is an office administrator. They both have RRSPs, TSFAs, and savings. This, combined with their CPPs, OAS, and private pensions, ensures they will retain their current standard of living. The mortgage on their home will be paid off in three years.

They are reviewing their financial situation with a financial advisor primarily to build a consolidated picture of their assets. Elma's financial net worth is significantly larger than Susan's. As they move into retirement, both feel the need to draw equally from their respective resources.

Elma and Susan set to work creating a retirement vision.

Elma:
- Will continue working for three more years, after which she will accept temporary community leadership assignments. These assignments could be at her current office or at locations throughout the city.
- Will continue enjoying her pottery-making hobby. She also enjoys reading, particularly histories and biographies.
- Is currently being interviewed to direct two theatre productions for two community theatre groups.
- Plans to return to college to earn an advanced coaching diploma, permitting her to offer coaching services from her home and online.
- Has started an exercise regime consisting of walking in malls and hiking in nearby parks.

Susan:

- Will work ten years, then retire from full-time employment.
- Plans to continue accepting weekend gigs as a musician. She plans to volunteer within the musical community, possibly teaching children to play woodwinds.
- Has an interest in starting a exercise routine, possibly cycling.

Together, Elma and Susan enjoy entertaining their close friends, going to concerts and plays, travelling to wine tastings, and eating at high-end restaurants. Both have a bucket list and are proceeding to fulfill their respective listings. Two list items they both share is to travel to the North and South Poles and to run with the bulls in Pamplona, Spain.

When asked about the benefits of extensive planning for life after work, Elma and Susan replied:

- At the beginning, the process can be difficult — sensitive topics include money and sharing of assets, space needs, relationships with partner's family members, etc. Once they had started, they experienced an increased ease talking about all issues and how they can tackle them.
- Sharing and describing retirement plans, ideas, hopes, and dreams provided a platform for in-depth conversations with each other and close friends. It was valuable to learn their friends' thoughts, opinions, and ideas for improvement.
- They would recommend everyone forty-five and older to embrace holistic retirement planning.

Sam and Maria

Throughout Sam's life, his obsession was managing his tool and die business and amassing as much money as he could. For years, he worked twelve hours a day meeting clients and prospective clients, supervising the shop work, consulting with engineers and planners, and ensuring the office was run efficiently.

Sam's relationship with his wife, Maria, was distant and strained. Due to Sam's work schedule, Maria built herself an independent life that included volunteering in the children's ward of the local hospital, playing bridge at the community drop-in centre, taking oil painting classes, and visiting with a wide circle of friends. Maria also babysat her five grandchildren when they were young and oversaw the care of her aged mother.

Though Sam thought he'd work well into his seventies, his physician recently told him he has a mild heart condition and advised him to reduce his work schedule. The news shocked Sam. For several weeks, he was depressed. On the advice of a friend, he began to work with a retirement planning expert.

As a result of the discussions with his retirement expert, Sam began to cut back his hours at work, shift many of his responsibilities to his second-in-command, and create a realistic retirement plan.

Sam's retirement plan:
- As the sole owner of the tool and die business, Sam wants to sell the company to the employees. His thirty-five-year-old son, Terry, and forty-year-old daughter, Stephanie, are not interested in the business. Sam

wants to retain a fifteen percent ownership of the firm and will act as a consultant for the first two years, after which he will become a silent partner.

- Sam will work closely with a psychologist to learn how to establish more accepting relationships with his son and daughter and his four grandchildren. His relationships with Terry and Stephanie are strained and have been non-existent for long periods.

- Sam and Maria are planning social events together, including taking long walks and incorporating date nights into their weekly schedule. They have started planning vacations to exotic places such as Hawaii, Japan, and Morocco.

- Maria and Sam are now taking ballroom dance classes once a week, and through this activity, they are meeting people with the same interest. Also, they have become members of their local Probus club and are active in two hobby groups: wine tasting and bird-watching.

- Maria and Sam will be selling their city home in the next year and taking up residence at their cottage. They have already ensured medical care is available when they move and have agreed to transfer ownership of the cottage to Terry and Stephanie after their passing.

- With the assistance of his physician, Sam is now a

member of a gym and is following a physical fitness program designed to meet his needs, keeping in mind his health limitations. He is also consulting with a nutritionist and is following a healthy diet, which has given him increased energy and stamina.

- As part of his health regime, Sam has incorporated several relaxation techniques into his daily routine, including deep breathing and progressive muscle relaxation. He feels less tense and much more grounded.

- To regain his sense of overall worth, Sam is regularly attending his place of worship. He recognizes the importance of spirituality being a part of his health and well-being. Maria takes solace in her oil painting and communing with nature.

- Sam will continue to meet with his retirement planner to keep his plans on track and continue to plan for his retirement years that lie ahead. He finds working with a mentor one of the most rewarding experiences he's ever had. He and his planner share insights and experiences and ensure Sam will flourish by exploring different approaches while remaining in control of his retirement.

Chapter 19

You As a Mentor

Summary:
What is it like being someone's retirement mentor? You will share your knowledge, insights, and support to the mutual benefit of you and your mentee.

This chapter looks at various strategies for becoming a mentor.

As you succeed in retirement, you too may be approached to be someone's mentor. If so, the potential mentee probably admires what you are accomplishing in retirement and wishes to benefit from your counsel. When this happens, seek out information about the mentee. Ensure you will spend your time wisely before agreeing to become a mentor.

The following are some basic mentee features that might influence you in your decision whether to become a mentor:

1. **Having a plan.** It is essential for the mentee to have and be able to communicate a goal and plan for their retirement. The mentee should have already given some previous thought to what they want and some ideas about how to get there. As a mentor, you can advise and encourage, but you cannot create a retirement

plan for someone else. If the plan is to be successful for the mentee, it has to be their own.

2. **Bringing something to exchange.** The potential mentee should be able to show how the mentoring relationship would benefit you too. The exchange for you could be the mentee's enthusiasm to learn and willingness to try new ideas and approaches. They may be able to provide you with a different perspective on aspects of retirement that would enrich your own learning and retirement planning.

3. **Making a good impression.** When discussing a possible working relationship with a potential mentee, ask these questions: Does the individual make good eye contact with you? Do they demonstrate attentive body language? Are they clear in their communication in terms of how questions are phrased? Does the mentee describe problems and challenges constructively without whining?

At the end of the discussion, take a few minutes to assess how you feel. Decide whether this is a good fit for you. Will the two of you be able to work well together? Do you feel comfortable with the potential mentee? Do you want to mentor this person?

Well-functioning mentor/mentee relationships are rewarding for both people. It's an opportunity for you to share your insights and experience and for the mentee to flourish by exploring different approaches to retirement while remaining in control.

Chapter 20

Pets in Retirement

Summary:
In this chapter, we will evaluate the benefits and drawbacks of having pets in retirement.

There is also a case study and an exercise.

Pets are lovable sources of companionship at any age. Our pets are a part of the family, and in some cases these furry friends have a higher ranking than other family members.

As you enter retirement, your pet may be getting older with a life expectancy much shorter than your own. A common mistake made by retirees is immediately replacing Muffin, Mittens, or Buster without carefully evaluating the impact of the decision on their retirement plan. Consider a retiree who plans to travel, volunteer, and have hobbies outside the home. They now have a new pet — possibly a kitten or a puppy — and are limited because of the need to care for the animal. It might be difficult to leave it for weeks at a time, especially when travelling or going on vacation.

Family and friends are often reluctant to look after a pet, especially for long periods. The costs of kennelling can be high, not to mention the emotional aspects of leaving your pet in a strange place. If you wish to take your pet with you when you travel, you may find many hotels, inns, and bed and breakfasts that do not allow them.

Part of Miranda and Nelson's retirement plan was to take a major trip once a year. Spice, their Irish setter, was an important part of their family. Whenever they travelled, their neighbours would kindly take care of Spice, as they also had a dog the same age and the animals were friends.

Just before Miranda and Nelson's retirement, their neighbour's dog died. Everyone was saddened by the event, especially Spice, who missed her long-time companion. Much to Miranda and Nelson's surprise, their neighbours elected not to get another animal.

Two months later, Spice passed away from old age. Devastated and struggling to cope with their loss, Miranda and Nelson rushed out and bought a new dog, an Australian shepherd named Tucker. For the next three months, they were housebound caring for their new pet. In this time, Tucker became a beloved member of the family.

Comfortable with Tucker's development and training, Miranda and Nelson planned a trip to Greece. It was to be the trip of a lifetime. They assumed that their neighbours would care for Tucker while they were away. After finalizing plans and booking their tickets, they approached the neighbours to see if they would watch Tucker. The neighbours said no, as it would be too hard emotionally to have another dog in the house.

Before leaving for Greece, Miranda and Nelson placed Tucker in a kennel. Though they knew he would receive good care, they worried so much about Tucker's stay in a strange place that a lot of their enjoyment of Greece was lost and they regretted their decision to get another dog.

If you own a pet, there will come a time when you and your partner will face its passing. Prior to this happening, take time to discuss the advantages and disadvantages of obtaining another pet. Discuss your future retirement plans and determine if a pet is part of them. It is crucial to consider the commitment of owning another pet.

EXERCISE 27

Answer the following questions:

1. If our pet dies, would we want another? Why or why not?

_____

_____

_____

_____

_____

_____

_____

_____

2. What problems may stem from us getting a pet at this stage of our lives?

_____

_____

_____

_____

_____

_____

_____

_____

3. What changes in our lives would make us consider getting a pet in the future if we don't currently have one now?

_____

_____

_____

_____

_____

_____

_____

On the other hand, what happens to your pet if you are incapacitated, are hospitalized, or die? As a pet owner, you should have a plan for the care of your pet.

1. Arranging for short-term pet care. Try to find a friend or relative who is willing to take care of your pet for short periods brought on by illness or hospitalization.

2. Arranging short-term care at a shelter or charitable organization. In the event of your hospitalization, provide the shelter or charitable organization with written instructions and permission for taking care of your pet.

3. Designating caregivers. Find a friend or relative who is willing to take your pet and give it a good home if something should happen to you.

4. Providing funds for pet care. You may choose to leave a sum of money for your pet's designated caregiver along with instructions that it is to be used for the care of the animal.

5. Designating a shelter. If you cannot find a friend or relative willing to take your pet, look for a charitable organization whose function is to care for or place companion animals.

6. Providing for euthanasia if caregivers cannot be found. While you may feel it's essential to protect your pet from mistreatment or a bad home, it is questionable whether a healthy pet's life should end by euthanasia when you die. Nevertheless, if you wish to provide for euthanasia, speak to your lawyer about specifying in your will that your pet is to be cared for by your executor or a friend for a specified period. Ask that this person attempt to find a good home for your pet. Indicate that they may euthanize your pet if they cannot locate a home after reasonable time and effort.

Appendix

A. **Financial Planning**
   1. **Canada Pension Plan/Québec Pension Plan (CPP/QPP) — Canada**
   2. **Old Age Security (OAS) — Canada**
   3. **Social Security — US**
   4. **Company Pension Plans and Benefits**
   5. **Savings Plans, Retirement Accounts, and Other Assets**
B. **Relationships Expanded**
   1. **Caring for Elderly Parents**
   2. **Parenting in Retirement**
   3. **Step-Grandparenting**
   4. **Family Challenges**
   5. **Sex**
   6. **Increasing the Romance**

C. **Websites for Seniors**

1. Canada Pension Plan/Québec Pension plan (CPP/QPP) — Canada

For 2019, the maximum CPP/QPP retirement benefit for new recipients age sixty-five is $1,154.58 per month. You should determine how much you might receive from CPP/QPP from ages sixty through sixty-five and determine whether it makes economic sense to collect your CPP/QPP before age sixty-five. Your financial advisor or accountant will be able to assist with your answer.

I recommend you submit your application for CPP/QPP as early as twelve months before the month in which you want your pension to begin. To qualify for the monthly CPP/QPP pension, you must meet one of the following criteria:

1. You are sixty-five years of age or older.
2. You are between sixty and sixty-five years of age and have stopped working or have earnings from work below the maximum CPP/QPP retirement pension for two consecutive months.

If you elect to receive your pension at age sixty, your monthly payment will be thirty-six percent less than if you had taken it at sixty-five. If you take your pension after sixty-five, your monthly amount may be larger, by up to forty-two percent at age seventy.

For information on CPP, call:
In Canada or the US
1-800-277-9914 (English)
1-800-277-9915 (French)
or visit www.canada.ca/en/services/benefits/
publicpensions/cpp.html

For information on QPP, call:
In Canada or the US
1-800-463-5185
or visit www.rrq.gouv.qc.ca/en/programmes/regime_rentes/

2. Old Age Security (OAS) — Canada

OAS is a basic benefit paid to all Canadians who are sixty-five and older and meet certain Canadian residency requirements. The maximum monthly payment amount is $601.45 per month. Depending on other income, you might have to give some or all of OAS back.

To apply for OAS, you can submit your application up to twelve months before you turn sixty-five. If you are already sixty-five or older, send in your application as soon as possible so you won't lose any more payments.

For information on OAS, call:
In Canada or the US
1-800-277-9914 (English)
1-800-277-9915 (French)
or visit www.canada.ca/en/services/benefits/publicpensions/cpp/old-age-security.html

3. Social Security — US

The average American receives a portion of retirement income from Social Security. To qualify for Social Security retirement benefits, you need a certain number of credits. If you were born in 1929 or later, you need forty credits, which represents ten years of work. Your benefit payment amount is based on how much you earned during your working career. Higher lifetime earnings result in higher benefits.

In 2019, the maximum benefit at age sixty-five is $2,757 per month. If you retire at age sixty-two, the earliest possible retirement age for Social Security, the maximum benefit in 2019 is $2,209 per month. If you retire at age seventy, the maximum benefit in 2019 is $3,770 per month.

Supplemental Security Income (SSI)
SSI is an income supplement program available through Social Security. It is designed to help disabled adults and children with little or no income. It provides benefit payments to meet basic needs for food, clothing, and shelter.

For more information on Social Security, call:
1-800-772-1213
or visit www.socialsecurity.gov

4. Company Pension Plans and Benefits

Now it's time to review your company pension plan and benefits. Company plans are as varied as the companies that offer them. Become familiar with your company's plan. See what it offers and how it can add to your other retirement income sources.

At the same time, ask about the continuance of your company life insurance, medical, health, and dental benefits when you retire.

Finally, if you have worked in another country, check with that country's pension authorities to determine your eligibility for a government pension.

5. Savings Plans, Retirement Accounts, and Other Assets

Determine what you have in savings, your RRSPs or 401(k), and locked-in retirement accounts (LIRAs). List all income from non-registered investments as well. Be sure to look at interest from personal savings accounts and interest, dividends, and redemptions from GICs, mutual funds, stocks, and bonds. Don't forget the conversion of some equity, income from business assets and real estate, and the liquidation of personal assets.

6. Tips for Living on a Budget

The following are several tips on how to live on a budget:

- **Don't dump unaccounted-for expense dollars into miscellaneous.** The more specific your tracking, the easier it is to find those extras that are the least painful to cut. Do you dine out at breakfast or lunch on workdays? Brown-bagging a few of those meals can mean real savings. Just $2 a day means an extra $520 at the end of the year. Save $5 a day, and you'll have $1,300.

- **Pay yourself first.** When you pay your bills, set aside some money to deposit into your savings account. Paying yourself $50 each month becomes $600 a year in savings.

- **Consolidate your debts.** You may be able to take care of several small loans or credit card bills with one larger loan at a lower interest rate. You can also use some of your savings to pay off those debts if the interest charges are higher than the interest earned from your savings.

- **Reduce your insurance premiums.** Accept a higher deductible or cancel collision coverage on an older vehicle you may not repair if in an accident.

- **Leave room in your plans for rewards.** Don't eliminate all the fun expenses or you'll lose your motivation to stick to your cash plan. Instead, try to tone down or cut back on some forms of entertainment or recreation. For example, play one round of golf a week rather than two or host get-togethers with friends at home rather than go to a restaurant.

- **Keep paying paid-off debts.** After you make your final payment on your car or mortgage, keep writing those monthly checks, but start putting the money into your savings account.

EXERCISE 28

These are the financial changes I will make to help obtain my retirement vision and goals.

_____

_____

_____

_____

_____

_____

_____

_____

B. Relationships Expanded
1. Caring for Elderly Parents

Building on what we discussed in Chapter 8: Choosing Where to Live is the likely need for caring for an aging parent and all the questions that go along with it. Can you get them help at home? If so, how do you go about doing that? Do they need to go into a retirement or nursing home? What about your home? Do you have enough space? More importantly, do you and your partner want them moving in with you?

i.   Home Care

There may come a time in your retired life that your or your partner's parents are no longer able to live a happy, safe, and healthy lifestyle in their place of residence. Depending on your family circumstances, you may be the one faced with obtaining care for them. When accepting this challenge, take the time to find the most suitable person to assist with the care and comfort of your loved one. Here are steps to finding the right candidate.

Step 1
Advertise. A sample ad could read as follows: "Female needed part-time for personal care and housekeeping for an older disabled woman. Flexible hours. Call 416-555-1234 after 7 p.m."

Step 2
Screen the candidates. Before arranging an interview, create a job description and make sure to ask a few questions so that the person applying understands the primary duties and schedule. This will give you insight into the prospective employee's experience and training. Also, be ready to provide information such as:
- How many hours of work are needed (total per week or month)
- What days and times are required
- Specific duties including driving, if applicable
- Salary and benefits, frequency of pay
- Other specifics (e.g., non-smoker, must speak the same language your parent speaks, etc.)

Step 3
Interview candidates. Interviewing is key in your hiring process. This is where you ask detailed questions and begin to evaluate which candidate is best suited for the

job. Use the following questions as your guide:

- Tell me a little about yourself, your interests, and hobbies.
- How do you feel about working with an elderly or disabled person?
- Where have you worked before? Do you have experience working with an elderly or disabled person?
- Do you know about _____? (Ask about a relevant illness or condition.)
- Do you have any health or physical problems that might hinder you on the job? (Ask about lifting, bending, ability to drive, etc.)
- What other obligations do you have, such as school or a part-time job, that will affect your schedule?
- Do you have a car? Would you be able to transport someone in a wheelchair?
- How do you handle someone who is upset, angry, or fearful?
- What made you choose this kind of work?
- How do you feel about smoking, drinking, or using drugs?
- Is there anything in the job description that you would not do?
- Do you have any questions about the job duties, schedule, or salary?
- Is there anything else you would like to add?
- Can you provide me with two work-related references and one personal reference?

Step 4
Evaluate the candidate. After interviewing a candidate,

take time to write down your impressions, concerns, and gut feelings. Try to do this immediately while the person is still fresh in your mind. Ask yourself:

- Did the person arrive on time?
- Did I have a good feeling about the person?
- Did we agree on the duties and schedule?
- Did the person provide the requested references?
- Did I tell the person when I would notify them?
- Was there anything about the person that made me uncomfortable?

Step 5

Check references. Once you have narrowed down your choices, be sure to check the background of each candidate. Use the following questions to check with previous employers:

- How long have you known the candidate?
- What was their position?
- What were the responsibilities of the job?
- What is your impression of them as a worker?
- Is the person reliable? Punctual?
- Did they show initiative or wait to be told what to do?
- Does the person listen well? Follow instructions?
- Is the person trustworthy?
- Do they show good common sense?
- Were there any problems on the job?
- Were you aware of any problems with drugs or alcohol?
- Would you recommend this person?

Step 6

Select the candidate and offer the position. Hiring a home care worker requires patience and trust. The time invested in screening candidates and checking references will greatly improve your chances of finding someone whose qualifications meet your caregiving needs.

Once you've hired your home care worker, ensure they have all the critical information and documentation that may be needed in an emergency, such as:

- Name and contact information of your parent's family doctor
- Health card number
- List of allergies
- List of medications
- Medical history
- Name and contact information of next of kin (home, work, and cell numbers)
- Name and contact information of the substitute decision maker — an individual appointed to make decisions should your parent be deemed incapable — or attorney for personal care
- Contact information for the power of attorney

ii. Nursing Home Care

Another possible solution is finding a nursing home for a parent who is no longer able to live on their own. Before making your decision, take the time to investigate the nursing homes available to determine the best facility given the finances and the need for comfort and service, for your loved one.

Use the following to assist you with your review of homes:

- Note the types and locations of nursing home alternatives.
- Are private and semi-private accommodations available?
- Do they have long-term care?
- What facilities are offered? (e.g., recreation, lounge, dining room, etc.)
- Check the staffing levels, including registered nurses and certified nursing assistants.
- What equipment is available? (e.g., adjustable beds and chairs, etc.)
- Check quality measures and standards.
- What are the visiting privileges?
- Are the safety plans including the fire evacuation procedures adequate?
- Is a doctor available day and night?
- Does the nursing home offer moving assistance?

Before deciding on a nursing home, check the ownership. Is it run by an independent nonprofit organization or a private company? Nonprofits may offer more one-on-one care than private operations. Talk to the home administrator about quality standards, inspections, and turnover of top-level staff members. Visit each home several times at different hours, including day and night. Is there a discernable difference in what you see at various times?

iii. Parents Moving In

Another option when determining care for a parent is to have them live with you. Before making this decision, survey your home. Would you need a self-contained suite or an additional bedroom? Does your property have enough space for an addition? What are the construction bylaws in your area? Consider the needs of your parent. Will climbing stairs be a problem? Is your basement suitable for a suite?

It's essential to recognize the costs associated with making renovations. According to contractors, costs for converting a basement into a fully contained suite can be as high as $50,000. A 500 square foot addition is in the neighbourhood of $85,000, and adding a single 150 square foot room to a house can be upwards of $10,000 to $15,000.

Even if your parent has no trouble with mobility now, think about their future needs. Things such as:

- Widened doorways to accommodate wheelchairs or walkers
- Levers instead of doorknobs to make opening doors easier
- Grab bars in bathrooms
- Showers instead of tubs for ease of access
- Enhanced lighting, especially in stairways, kitchens, and bathrooms
- Minimal stairs and level changes
- Stairs with closed risers
- Sturdy handrails
- Raised toilet seats for easier access

As part of your deliberations, you and your spouse should discuss what costs you will share with your parents and which costs are your parent's responsibility. For example, if you build a self-contained suite, how much money would you expect your parent to contribute to cover the costs?

Once your parent is occupying the suite, would you expect them to pay for their groceries, telephone, and cable? Do you expect them to share the costs of heat, electricity, water, and taxes?

The decision to hire a home care worker, place a loved one into a nursing home, or have a parent come live with you is not an easy one. The more you and your partner discuss the options in an open and trusting way, the better the decision and its acceptance will be. Include your parent in the discussions, and get their suggestions. Try not to make such an important decision quickly or emotionally. Give yourself time to reflect on the possibilities and outcomes. Be sure to consult with family members and knowledgeable community advisers before making your final decision. For further information, visit www.cdnhomecare.ca or www.usahomecare.net.

EXERCISE 29

Considering the age and health of your parents, what actions do you envision occurring in the next five years? Will your parents or your spouse's parents be able to live on their own or will they require home care or nursing care? Would or could you and your spouse have a parent share your home?

Notes

_____

_____

_____

_____

_____

_____

_____

_____

2. Parenting in Retirement

Parenting in retirement can raise many issues. Once retired, you may find yourself re-examining many areas of your life, including the relationships you have with your children. Many retirees have adult children who run their own lives with their respective families.

Perhaps you wish to spend more time with your children and grandchildren, as you take great pride and enjoyment from being with them. This is all well and good as long as your children support this decision. However, time is precious to most adult children. Most adults keep busy with working, raising children, keeping a home and yard, maintaining relationships with friends, and all the other aspects of daily life. If not carefully thought out, this is where a potential clash can occur. If you want to be with your children and grandchildren more often, but your children don't share the same idea, this may result in disappointment and hard feelings.

Another potential difficulty that sometimes arises between retirees and their children is that an adult child may feel they can call upon you at a moment's notice. There's always a need for a good babysitter or someone to help with tasks such as painting or yard work. Beyond your time, your adult child may also see you as a source for financial help. You have a pension, your mortgage is paid off, and you have extra cash to spend on such things as clothes and sports fees for your grandchildren. They may expect you to pick up the tab at restaurants or help with their car or house payments.

To avoid many of these problems, you and your children need to have a discussion about what you expect from each other. Explore and understand each other's expectations, and when either side wants too much, the other should have the freedom to say, "Wait a minute. Let's talk about this."

The same holds true with your spouse or partner. As a retired couple, you need to find a delicate balance where you can have healthy, loving relationships with your adult children without treading on their independence. This means respecting their space and right to say, "Sorry, Mom and Dad, this is not a good time for you to come over."

You and your spouse can help each other achieve the correct balance of time and support regarding your adult children. One partner may feel the other tends to spend too much or too little time with the children and grandchildren and may suggest moderation.

Nora and Roger have recently retired. They have two daughters, Terry and Helen. Terry and her husband, Steve, live in town, and Helen lives in a city four hundred kilometres away. Terry and Helen each have two small children who are very active in various activities, including swimming, soccer, and hockey. Time is precious, as every minute is taken up by work, family, and friends.

When Nora and Roger were employed with their respective companies, they regularly visited with Terry, Steve, and the kids every two or three weeks. Due to the distance, the visits were less frequent with Helen and her children.

Now that Nora and Roger are retired, they have suggested more frequent visits, like once or twice a week with Terry and Steve, and once every three weeks with Helen. When they proposed this plan, it was not received with enthusiasm, as it meant a major disruption to their children's and grandchildren's existing schedules. After some honest discussion, they revised the plan to visits once every two weeks with Terry and Steve and once every six weeks with Helen and her family. Everyone agreed to the arrangement and agreed to regularly review the frequency of visits to ensure their workability.

EXERCISE 30

List what you want in retirement from your relationships with your children and grandchildren. What does your partner want?

Regarding our children and grandchildren:

What do I want?   What does my partner want?

One day a week together   *As much time as possible together*

_____

_____

_____

_____

_____

_____

_____

_____

Answer the following questions regarding parenting and children:

1. Do we and the children understand each another's expectations?

_____

_____

_____

_____

_____

_____

_____

_____

2. Do any of our expectations need to be altered?

_____

_____

_____

_____

_____

_____

_____

_____

3. Are there any areas of disagreement between us as a
    couple about parenting? If so, how might these be re-
    solved?

_____

_____

_____

_____

_____

_____

_____

_____

4. How much involvement, and what kind, do we want with our grandchildren? What needs to change to achieve this?

_____

_____

_____

_____

_____

_____

_____

5. Are there any areas of disagreement between us as a couple about grandparenting? If so, how might these be resolved?

_____

_____

_____

_____

_____

_____

_____

Action plan

_____

_____

_____

_____

_____

_____

_____

3. Step-Grandparenting

In today's world, blended families are becoming increasingly common. Many people become a step-grandparent when they or their children remarry someone who already has children.

Establishing a relationship with a step-grandchild isn't easy. Sometimes, the child's parent or the child won't accept you. Sometimes, neither of them will. If this situation presents itself, don't try to demand acceptance. Instead take the long view that the relationship needs time to form for them to see you as a special person in their life.

Don't push to be called "Granddad" or "Grandma." You may have to accept being called by your first name or uncle/aunt. Furthermore, don't reprimand the child for anything unless there is a need for physical safety. Leave discipline to the biological grandparent or the child's parent(s).

As for the biological grandparents, recognize there is a natural bond between them and their grandchild. Respect that bond and try to foster it rather than compete with it. Don't try to outdo the biological grandparent's Christmas or birthday gifts. Rather, work with your step-grandchild and their parents to create an atmosphere where everyone accepts you, your love, and your kindness.

EXERCISE 31

If you have step-grandchildren, list the steps can you take to better build a loving relationship and, at the same time, respect the needs and feelings of the biological grandparents.

I accept being called Uncle Jack. I will treat my step-grandchildren the same way I treat my biological grandchildren. I will spend the same amount of money on gifts for both my step-grandchildren and grandchildren.

_____

_____

_____

_____

_____

_____

_____

4. Family Challenges

As you move forward into retirement, there will be uncomfortable situations. Whether it's the illness of an elderly parent, divorce amongst your children, or one of them moving back home, it is vital that you and your partner recognize the importance of having a unified approach to problem-solving. If you and your spouse disagree on how to tackle problems, your divided thinking may act as a wedge between the two of you, resulting in a damaged relationship.

Some of the more common family challenges are:

- The return of an adult child after a divorce
- A married child wanting to borrow large sums of money
- The serious illness of a parent
- The request for extensive babysitting

By not foreseeing and discussing potential problems, you might make quick decisions that one of you might not support. Critical decisions made in the heat of the moment may tear at your relationship as a couple at a time in your lives when you're looking forward to more peaceful times together.

I recommended you and your spouse play the "what if?" game to avoid conflict and split decisions:

- What if our twenty-six-year-old daughter wants to move back in with us to save money for a down payment on a house? What will our answer be?
- What if our married son wants to borrow money? How will we handle the situation?
- What if Mom gets seriously ill? Who in the family should discuss nursing home options with her?

By talking about various likelihoods, you and your partner can determine the best action for all concerned without actually facing the situation. Weigh the pros and cons of each possible solution and rationally consider the merits of each before formulating an action plan. If and when the event occurs, the two of you will have already worked out a strategy and can demonstrate a unified approach, which will add to your overall strength as a couple.

Nola and her husband, Jerome, have a thirty-year-old son named Norm. He is single and has a good education but has problems holding a job for more than twelve months. He finds something wrong with every job, whether it's the people, the pay, the hours, the lack of prospects, and the list goes on.

When Norm quits a job, he usually either knocks on the door of his older brother or calls Nola and Jerome to put him up. Nola and Jerome are approaching retirement, and are looking forward to a life of relaxation. However, there is a potential problem of the returning Norm.

As part of their retirement planning, Nola and Jerome discussed what they would do the next time Norm comes knocking. After reviewing the options, they agreed to permit Norm to stay for a maximum of one week and give him $500. They would tell Norm it was a one-time gift and that he is on his own the next time he leaves a job and should not expect room, board, or financial help. Both Nola and Jerome are satisfied with their joint decision and are now prepared to face the situation, knowing they are both on the same page.

EXERCISE 32

With your spouse, list the potential problems or questions that may arise in the future. Together, determine the action you will take if and when the problems occur.

Potential Problems

Divorce of our daughter Kim

Potential Solutions

Help Kim financially for a maximum of three months

_____	_____
_____	_____
_____	_____
_____	_____
_____	_____
_____	_____

5. Sex

Sex is a vital aspect of living and relationships. Throughout our lives, we all have thought about, dreamed about, and practiced sex. It is a significant component of any vibrant relationship. Unfortunately, many retirees believe that sex is something they have to forget about, as it is meant for younger people. The good news is nothing can be further from the truth!

Why do older people see sex as something for the young? It's simple. Over time, we have allowed ourselves to be influenced by myths and falsehoods. For instance, one myth is that biology has established a mandatory age for sexual retirement among men. This is completely inaccurate. Some men over ninety are still potent.

Age Group	Percentage of Adults Still Sexually Active
57-64	73 percent
64-75	53 percent
75-85	26 percent

Source: *New England Journal of Medicine,* August 23, 2007, volume 357

Another myth suggests that people suffering from heart disease should not engage in sex due to the exertion required. Cardiac energy expenditure during a sexual climax is about equal to climbing two flights of stairs.

If you have questions about your sexual ability, see your physician. It's essential for you to appreciate the importance of sexual activity and how you can continue to enjoy this aspect of your retirement life.

Don't let others, such as your children, influence your views about sex. One of the primary oppositions to sexual freedom among seniors comes from adult children who have already accepted greater freedoms for themselves.

Even though some retired men report difficulties with sexual activity due to erectile deficiency (ED) and some women suffer from lower sexual desire, most couples continue to enjoy regular intimacy. To increase your sexual prowess, stop smoking, engage in regular exercise, control your weight, drink alcohol in moderation, and eat right. Taking these steps will help protect your heart and make you healthier overall, but they will also increase your sexual drive and satisfaction.

6. Increasing the Romance

It's your unlimited power to care and to love that can make the biggest difference in the quality of your life.
— Tony Robbins

Besides sex, there is another aspect of love we sometimes overlook or take for granted. That is enjoying the company of our partner, the romance of being together. This could be a candlelit dinner, a walk in the park, holding hands, snuggling while watching television, or giving your partner a back rub. It's the ability to please your spouse by doing little things that bring you both pleasure and closeness. People who are wise in years have a way of making the most of this so-called second language of love. In retirement, you and your partner have the time and hopefully the inclination to participate in this incredibly romantic and fulfilling demonstration of affection.

Some ways to increase the romance with your partner include the following:

- Pay attention to your spouse when they mention an interest in things such as books, movies, music, and theatrical productions. These can be gift ideas for Christmas, birthdays, or anniversaries, or simply for "I love you" gifts.
- Offer to give your partner a back rub or foot massage. Make your offer frequently and sincerely.
- Leave cards, letters, or notes expressing your love. When you call or email, end the conversation or note with an "I love you."

- Regularly pamper and spoil your spouse. Make their coffee or tea in the morning, let them sleep in, or offer to do one of their chores such as doing the dishes or washing the car.
- Have your spouse's favourite music playing when they return home.
- When the two of you are in the company of others, make an effort to praise your spouse and how you appreciate everything they do.
- Make your spouse's favourite meal.
- Celebrate your time together with special lunches, surprise trips, and date nights.

Wake up each morning and ask yourself, "What can I do to make my spouse feel special today?" Use your imagination and vary your actions. Your spouse will thoroughly enjoy your tenderness and in all likelihood will respond in kind. Concentrating on the needs of your spouse, and vice versa, is a wonderful way to proceed through your retirement years.

Robert retired from his job at the age of sixty-three, and his wife, Helen, continued working at a local insurance office. Upon his retirement, Robert agreed to do the housework, yard maintenance, and grocery shopping.

When Helen returns home after a busy day, Robert ensures the house is clean and presentable. He also has ready a glass of Helen's favourite sherry, and he makes sure to prepare the evening meal and have it in the oven. Often, Robert offers to rub Helen's back and lights one of her scented candles.

Helen very much appreciates Robert's attention. She reciprocates by making him his favourite breakfast and ironing his shirts on her days off. They enjoy providing each other with attention, as they please each other and they both feel appreciated. They agree that their love for each other is increasing as they age, and they are looking forward to spending the rest of their lives in each other's company.

EXERCISE 33

What I can do for my partner?

_____

_____

_____

_____

_____

_____

_____

What can my partner do for me?

_____

_____

_____

_____

_____

_____

_____

C. Websites for Seniors

The following are resources you may find useful in retirement.

Senior Dating
www.seniorpeoplemeet.com

Managing Finances
www.canada.ca/en/services/benefits/publicpensions/
    cpp.html
www.ssa.gov/benefits/retirement/

Companion Care Services
www.homewellseniorcare.com
www.visitingangels.com

Hospital Sitting Services
www.careindeed.com/hospital-sitting

Finding a Place to Live
www.aplaceformom.com

Personal Care Services
www.seniorhelpers.ca

Grocery Delivery
www.amazon.ca/grocery

Downsizing
www.neat4ever.ca

Home and Property Maintenance
www.helpmyhomeplease.com

Driving and Transportation
www.mytransitplanner.com

Legal Assistance
www.advocacycentreelderly.org

Meal Delivery
www.feedmore.org/meals-on-wheels

Nursing Services
www.nursenextdoor.com

CPSIA information can be obtained
at www.ICGtesting.com
Printed in the USA
LVHW080518190919
631535LV00001B/1/P

9 781554 832354